Long Distance Walks

Volume Three

THE PEAK

by

TONY WIMBUSH

Acknowledgments

John Allen – Photography.

Dave Jeffery – Advice.

Ethna Boldison – Typing.

Ian Grant and the Rucksack Club – permission to quote from Club Journals.

Secker and Warburg – quotations and information from *High Peak* by Eric Byne and Geoffrey Sutton.

Diadem Books – quotation from *Big Walks* by K. Wilson and R. Gilbert.

Bob Tait, Geoff Bell, John Corfield, Neil Turner, Geoffrey Carr, Anthony Hewitt, Brian Hickling, Alan Earnshaw, John Merrill, D. E. Wilkins, Haydn Morris, Peter Hobson, T. P. Rogers, G. M. Rogers, Norman Witter, Roland Price, M. W. Smith, T. Peploe, Peak Park Joint Planning Board; Cheshire, Derbyshire, South Yorkshire and Nottinghamshire County Councils – information and assistance.

The Dalesman Publishing Company Ltd.,
Clapham, via Lancaster, LA2 8EB

First published 1983
© Tony Wimbush 1983

Cover photograph – Edale (John M. Brentnell)
Title page – Kinder Downfall (John Allen)

Printed by Alf Smith & Co., Bradford.

Contents

PREFACE 5
INTRODUCTION 6
HIGH PEAK CLASSICS 7
Marsden-Edale 8
Derwent Watershed 10
Colne to Rowsley 11
Peakland Horseshoe 12
Tan Hill Inn to Cat and Fiddle Inn 13
Other Walks 14

ANYTIME CHALLENGE WALKS 15
Bog Dodgers Way 17
Saddleworth Five Trig Points Walk 19
Ten Reservoirs Walk 21
Limey Way 23
Cal-Der-Went Walk 25
Peakland Heritage Walk 27
Leek Moors 14-400's Walk 29
New Five Trig Points Walk 32
Ancient Relics Walk 33
Cuckoo Walk 34
Classic Walks 35
Gritstone Edge Walk 35
Trail Blazer Challenge Walk 36
Three Feathers Walks 36

CHALLENGE EVENTS AND FELL RACES 37
High Peak Marathon 39
Bullock Smithy Hike 41
Four Inns Walk 43
Masters Hike 45
Edale Skyline Fell Race 47
Marsden-Edale Trog Fell Race 49
Bog Dodgers Event 49
Wild Ways Walk 50
YHA Peak Marathons 50
Rotherham Round Walk 51
Peakland Heritage Event 51
Peakland Hundred 52
Bolsover District Walk 52
Boscobel Walk 52

OFFICIAL LONG DISTANCE FOOTPATHS AND
RECREATIONAL PATHS 53
Pennine Way 55
Peakland Way 58
Derbyshire Gritstone Way 61
Derbyshire Boundary Walk 63
White Peak Way 63

Paths in adjacent areas
Sandstone Trail 64
Gritstone Trail 64
Nottinghamshire Heritage Way 65
Robin Hood Way 65
Mow Cop Spur Trail 65
Staffordshire Way 66

Peakland Trails
Tissington Trail 67
High Peak Trail 67
Monsal Trail 67
Sett Valley Trail 67

Peakland Trackways 68

GENERAL NOTES 69
Types of Long Distance Walking 70
Format of Walk Description 71
Safety on open challenge walks 71
Sponsored walks 72
Equipment for challenge walks 72
Guidelines on eating and drinking 73
Peak District National Park 74
Access to Open Country 75
Public Transport 77
Countryside Commission 77
Local Authorities 78
Organisations 79

Note: The inclusion of a route in this book should not be taken as implying a legal right of way or access.

Preface

THE PEAK overflows with a wealth of natural scenery for all to share and enjoy; in 1951 it was designated as Britain's first National Park. As long ago as 1966 it was recognised as one of the most valued and outstanding landscapes in Western Europe when it was awarded the Council of Europe's first Diploma in Conservation. Yet the Peak still remains vulnerable, National Park status guaranteeing very little, despite the fine work of the Park authority. Firstly there are the pressures of modern industries which threaten to erode a priceless national asset for short term economic expediency. But what is of more concern here is that the wild and delicate landscape of the Peak is vulnerable to the pressures of people, and of walkers. The damage done by the Lyke Wake Walk across the North York Moors, and in the Yorkshire Dales by the Three Peaks Walk is there for all to see, both in the widespread erosion and in local relationships. Short sections of the Pennine Way in the Peak have suffered a similar fate — so long distance paths and challenge walks can bring problems. There is now a full and varied selection of walks in the Peak as this survey shows. Helping to introduce people to the rewards of long distance walking is beneficial but perhaps the Peak has now reached saturation point; perhaps there is more to be lost than to be gained from promoting further routes. There should always be scope for walkers to devise their own challenges without somewhere having to follow in the footsteps of others. Surely it would be a sad day indeed if the proliferation of walks was to diminish the very beauty, solitude and challenge which was initially sought.

Tony Wimbush
March 1983

DERWENT EDGE

Introduction

*The man who never was lost
never went very far.*
G. H. B. Ward,
founder of the Sheffield Clarion Club.

WHILE there are many books for today's walker, few deal exclusively with the more adventurous and challenging forms of walking. This book explores the opportunities within the Peak from the turn of the century to the present day. No other region in Britain can claim such an outstanding tradition of long distance walking with such a gallery of legendary figures. Perhaps this is not surprising when you consider that it is flanked on nearly all sides by large industrial cities. Manchester and Sheffield are on the doorstep while Derby, Stoke, Nottingham and the towns of West Yorkshire are not far away. It was inevitable that the Peak should become the focus of attention and a breath of fresh air to these populations, especially with a rail network to give such easy access.

Many of the most significant developments in the outdoor and conservation movements have centred on the Peak. First came the emergence of walking as a sport and recreation with the formation of the first rambling clubs. Among them, both founded in 1902, were the Sheffield Clarion Club and the Rucksack Club which has continued to dominate the Peakland long distance walking scene for most of the century. Then followed the confrontation with gamekeepers protecting the interests of a feudal system of land ownership. This eventually culminated in the much publicised 1932 Kinder Mass Trespass and the battle for effective legislation. Out of this came the Peak District National Park, designated in 1951, the first in the country, and later in 1965 the Pennine Way, our first long distance footpath. The Park is administered by the Peak Park Joint Planning Board who have the task of preserving and enhancing its natural beauty as well as promoting its enjoyment by the public. Within the 542 square miles of the Peak is a rich diversity of scenery. In the north is the Dark Peak, harsh gritstone moorland with a wild and fascinating beauty. To the south is the White Peak, a country of rolling limestone plains, soft wooded dales and gentle rivers. Few areas can combine such variety and challenge ranging from long days out for the casual rambler to epic tests of mental and physical endurance for the trained athlete.

The High Peak Classics

Marsden — Edale	25 miles	(40 km)
Derwent Watershed	37½ miles	(60 km)
Colne — Rowsley	73 miles	(117 km)
Peakland Horseshoe	60 miles	(96 km)
Tan Hill Inn to Cat and Fiddle Inn	120 miles	(193 km)

The High Peak Classics have been well documented by Eric Byne and Geoffrey Sutton in their authoritative account of walking and climbing in the Peak. Spanning over half a century these walks tell something of the long tradition of Peakland walking. They not only provide excellent routes but, more important, perpetuate the spirit of adventurous endeavour which inspired them; the mark of a true classic.

Marsden — Edale

Our theme is the men who introduced a new sport to the Peak, the men who developed it, and the district as it seemed to them. It has always encouraged men and women of independent spirit. Where the deer once bounded away at the movement of Lincoln green in the thicket, stocky figures tramp by in corduroys and anoraks. Almost everything has changed except the moors and the wind and the unruly spirit of freedom it blows into those who know them.

from 'High Peak', Eric Byne and Geoffrey Sutton, 1966.

Start — Marsden   **Finish — Edale**
Distance — 25 miles (40 km)
Maps — O.S. Peak District Tourist (one inch) O.S. sheet 110 (1:50,000).
       Dark Peak Outdoor Leisure Map (1:25,000)

Introduction: This is the earliest and one of the best known bogtrots in the High Peak. Developed in 1902, the walk is associated with the legendary 'Colonel' Dawson although he himself credited it to a Ross Evans. The railway stations at Marsden and Edale provided a natural line for this formidable moorland traverse of the three main plateaux of Black Hill, Bleaklow and Kinderscout. The route allows numerous variations; all provide a classic day's outing across the roof of the Peak.

Fell Race: A fell race is held annually in December. See page 49

References: *High Peak,* Byne and Sutton (Secker and Warburg, 1966) *The Big Walks,* K. Wilson and R. Gilbert (Diadem Books, 1980).

Route Outline and Log:

No	Grid Ref.	Location	Height feet	Distance mls	km	2½ mph Pace	Date
1	047 115	Marsden	600	0	0	0	....
2	076 072	Wessenden Head	1450	4	6	1.35	....
3	073 993	Crowden	700	11	18	4.25	....
4	088 929	Snake Road	1650	18	29	7.10	....
5	123 860	Edale	850	25	40	10.00	....
						Total time	....

ROUTE SECTION

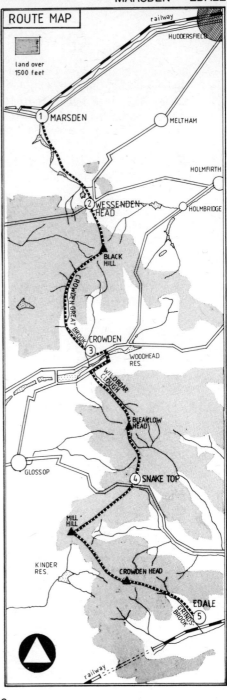

9

Derwent Watershed

Start and Finish — Yorkshire Bridge, Bamford
Distance — 37½ miles (60km)
Maps — O.S. Peak District Tourist (one inch) O.S. sheet 110 (1:50,000)
       Dark Peak Outdoor Leisure Map (1:25,000)
Origin — Eustace Thomas, Rucksack Club, 1918

Description: There are probably no better recommendations for this walk than that by Phil Cooper in *The Big Walks:-*

So there it is, the best, boggiest, bleakest, roughest, toughest, loneliest, wettest parts of the Peak District all brought into a day's walk encircling the headwaters of a fine river.

Just add some mist and rain and you have a circuit to stretch the stamina and navigation of the strongest bogtrotters. Along with Norman Bragg, Eustace Thomas inaugurated the route in 11 hours 39 minutes. He later went on to establish a new Lake District Fell Walking Record in 1922 following on from Cecil Dawson's record of 1916 which apparently was not nationally recognised. Today the route is best known in the form of the annual High Peak Marathon, see page 39 for details. The fastest time for the Watershed stands at 8 hours 15 minutes by Mike Cudahy of the Rucksack Club.

Route Outline: Yorkshire Bridge — Win Hill, — Lose Hill, — Rushup Edge, — Brown Knoll — Edale Cross — Kinder Downfall — Mill Hill — Ashop Head — Snake Road — Bleaklow Head — Bleaalow Stones — Swain's Head — Rocking Stones — Margery Hill — Strines Edge — High Neb — Yorkshire Bridge.

BLEAKLOW STONES

Colne to Rowsley

Start — Colne
Distance — 73 miles (117 km)

Finish — Rowsley
Maps — O.S. sheets 103, 109, 110, 119 (1:50,000

Origin — Fred Heardman, Rucksack Club, 1926

Description: The Marsden — Edale Walk provided the backbone of a number of longer expeditions including the Colne to Edale, the more popular 50 mile Colne to Buxton and the Colne to Ashbourne. None of these have achieved the notoriety of the Colne to Rowsley Walk which took a more easterly route. Inaugurated by Fred Heardman, and John Firth Brown, in 27 hours 30 minutes this was just one of his many notable achievements in his long and distinguished career dedicated to walking and conservation in the Peak District. The Colne — Rowsley Walk has since been repeated on numerous occasions and, as recently as 1982, Mike Cudahy of the Rucksack Club recorded a time of 11 hours 45 minutes. The following colourful extract from the 1937 Rucksack Club Journal probably echoes the sentiments of a good many of these attempts.

I don't think we cared very much. It all seemed so senseless – 2 am, darkness, mist drizzle – what a hopeless prospect with one's whole being yearning for a good warm bed. We left the road and floundered over rough squelchy moorland on to Black Hill. The mist was so thick, the darkness so intense, and our single light so inadequate that we seemed to make hardly any progress. It was impossible, too, to keep any sense of direction. I don't think I have ever felt more completely fed up than I did at that time. We seemed to be getting nowhere. What in heaven's name, I asked myself, had ever made me accept Bennett's cursed invitation? There seemed no sense or reason to it, What a fool I was – as if there isn't enough misery and suffering in life without looking for it like this! By this time too my light was getting dimmer and dimmer. Bennett disappeared down groughs with sickening frequency. It seemed simply hopeless – we couldn't go on like this indefinitely. My battery was running dry and the light was now failing almost entirely, so Bennett suggested that we transferred the bulb from my torch to his, since his battery had hardly been used. The idea worked, and in comparison the new beam shone like that of a motor headlight. Two minutes later it went out without warning. Bennett examined it by matchlight ... the battery had again been too strong for the bulb. Words failed me. The fellow was an electrical engineer ... I felt I had never witnessed such gross incompetence. And there we were, all through his carelessness, stranded without a light on a pitch-black night – misty, drizzly, inky – helpless in the middle of this wilderness.

Route Outline: Colne — Hebden Bridge — Marsden — Black Hill — Dunford Bridge — Cut Gate — Abbey Brook — Ladybower — Stanage — Hathersage — Longshaw — Froggatt Edge — Chatsworth — Rowsley.

Peakland Horseshoe

Start — Hen Cloud
Finish — Matlock
Distance — 60 miles (96 km)
Origin — Messrs Lambe and Sumner, Mountain Club, 1953
Map: O.S. Peak District Tourist (one inch).

Description: This walk is not particularly well known but does provide a route of interest and merit. The walk was inaugurated by R. E. (Larry) Lambe and John Sumner in August 1953 in a time of 37 hours 10 minutes during poor weather. At that time it was the toughest expedition entirely within the Peak District.

Route Outline: Hen Cloud — Combs Moss — Colbourne — Edale Cross — Kinder Downfall — Snake Road — Wainstones — Grinah Stones — Featherbed Moss — Abbey Brook — Stanage — Burbage Bridge — Higger Tor — Carl Wark — Longshaw — Froggatt Edge — Chatsworth — Beeley Moor — Matlock.

Tan Hill Inn to Cat and Fiddle Inn

Start — Tan Hill Inn, 1732 feet, County Durham (GR 897 067)
Finish — Cat and Fiddle Inn, 1690 feet, Cheshire (GR 001 719)
Distance — 120 miles (193 km)
Maps — O.S. sheets 91, 98, 104, 110, 119 (1:50,000)
Origin — Fred Heardman, Rucksack Club, 1952

Description: 1952 marked the fiftieth anniversary of the Rucksack Club so it was decided to hold a walk to celebrate the occasion. The result was this now infamous pub crawl down the Pennines to connect England's two highest inns with over 19,000 feet of ascent. V. J. Desmond completed the route in 54 hours 10 minutes with F. Williamson and T. Courtenay following on in 55 hours 40 minutes. The fastest recorded completion stands at 32 hours 20 minutes by Mike Cudahy.

That the spirit which inspired many of these early walks lives on within the Rucksack Club can be in little doubt as this introduction to an account of a recent winter Tan-Cat by John Richardson shows.

And what an exciting stimulating prospect sprang to mind: one hundred and fifteen or so miles of Pennines under English winter conditions – enough to turn one's blood to water.

There is probably a lot of truth in the widely held view that the miseries of longer walks shrink in the memory with the passage of time. Why then eleven years on, are my recollections of that first winter Tan Hill – Cat and Fiddle walk, ones of unending darkness? The only bits of daylight I can easily recall are times when we were resting. And why, since one Tan Hill – Cat and Fiddle walk is safely behind me, can I find no sufficient reason for non participation in another such banquet of self abuse?

Route Outline: Tan Hill Inn — Great Shunner Fell — Hawes — Semer Water — Buckden Pike — Great Whernside — Grassington — Rylstone Fell — Skipton — Cowling — Wolf Stones — Boulsworth Hill — Jackson's Ridge — Widdop reservoir — Todmorden — Blackstone Edge — Marsden — Black Hill — Stable Clough — Bleaklow — Snake Inn — Seal Stones — Kinder — Grindsbrook — Edale — Chapel Gate — Castle Naze — Long Hill — Goyt Bridge — Cat and Fiddle Inn.

Other Walks

This era also produced the following walks. Details are shown where available.

COLNE — BUXTON — 1904, 51 miles, by Cecil Dawson, Frank and Harry Summersgill.

COLNE — ASHBOURNE — 1919, by Harry Phillips.

THREE TUNNELS WALK — Cowburn, Woodhead and Diggle Tunnels, by Neil Ross.

THREE INNS WALK — Cat and Fiddle, Snake and Isle of Skye Inns, by Messrs Heardman, Berwick and Wild. Later extended to the Four Inns (see page 43).

THREE RIVERS WALK — Dane, Manifold and Dove, 50 miles, by R. E. Lambe in 1956, could be extended to include the Wye and Derwent.

Reference: *High Peak,* Eric Byne and Geoffrey Sutton, (Secker and Warburg, 1966).

Anytime Challenge Walks

EDALE VALLEY (J. ALLEN)

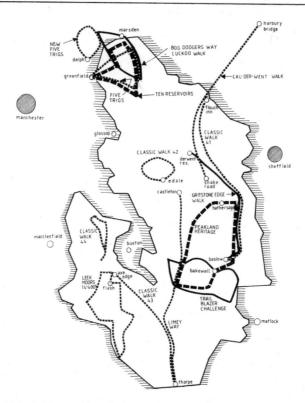

Bog Dodgers Way	22 miles	(35 km)
Saddleworth Five Trigs	20 miles	(32 km)
Ten Reservoirs Walk	22 miles	(35 km)
Limey Way	38 miles	(61 km)
Cal-Der-Went Walk	29 miles	(46 km)
Peakland Heritage Walk	36 miles	(58 km)
Leek Moors 14-400's	36 miles	(58 km)
New Five Trig Points Walk	18 miles	(29 km)
Ancient Relics Walk	25 miles	(40 km)
Cuckoo Walk	20 miles	(32 km)
Classic Walks 41 to 44	Various	
Gritstone Edge Walk	23 miles	(37 km)
Trail Blazer Challenge	25 miles	(40 km)
Three Feathers Walk	26 miles	(42 km)

Bog Dodgers Way

BOG DODGERS WAY

Start and Finish — Marsden Youth Hostel
Distance — 22 miles (35 km)
Ascent — 2250 feet (686m)
Time Limit — none
Maps — O.S. sheet 110 (1:50,000)
Origin — Major Alan Harrison, 1966

Introduction: A Major Alan Harrison of the Moorland Ambulance Corps originated this course in 1966 as the first anytime challenge walk in the Peak District. The Corps was disbanded in 1968 and along with it went the walk. Alan Earnshaw then revived the walk in 1978 and it has since emerged to be one of the most popular challenges in the area. The course is appropriately named, passing through some of the most notorious bogs in the Peak. Only well equipped walkers competent with map and compass should attempt this walk.

Completions: Total number of recorded completions — 3742. Fastest recorded completion — 3 hours 46 minutes by G. Orchard.

Challenge Event: An annual challenge event is held on the route in October, see page 49 for details.

Further Information: Send a large stamped addressed envelope for details of the route, badge and certificate to Alan Earnshaw, The Tourist Information Office, Brougham School, Penrith CA10 2AE.

Route Outline and Log:

No	Grid Ref	Location	Height Feet	Distance mls	Distance km	2½ mph pace	Date ....
1	048 112	Marsden YH	600	0	0	0	....
2	077 073	Isle of Skye	1450	4	6	1.35	....
3	095 041	Holme Moss	1750	7	11	2.50	....
4	053 063	A635	1500	10	16	4.00	....
5	020 097	Standedge	1250	15	24	6.00	....
6	002 122	A640	1350	18	29	7.10	....
7	048 112	Marsden YH	600	22	35	8.50	....
						Total time	....

BOG DODGERS WAY

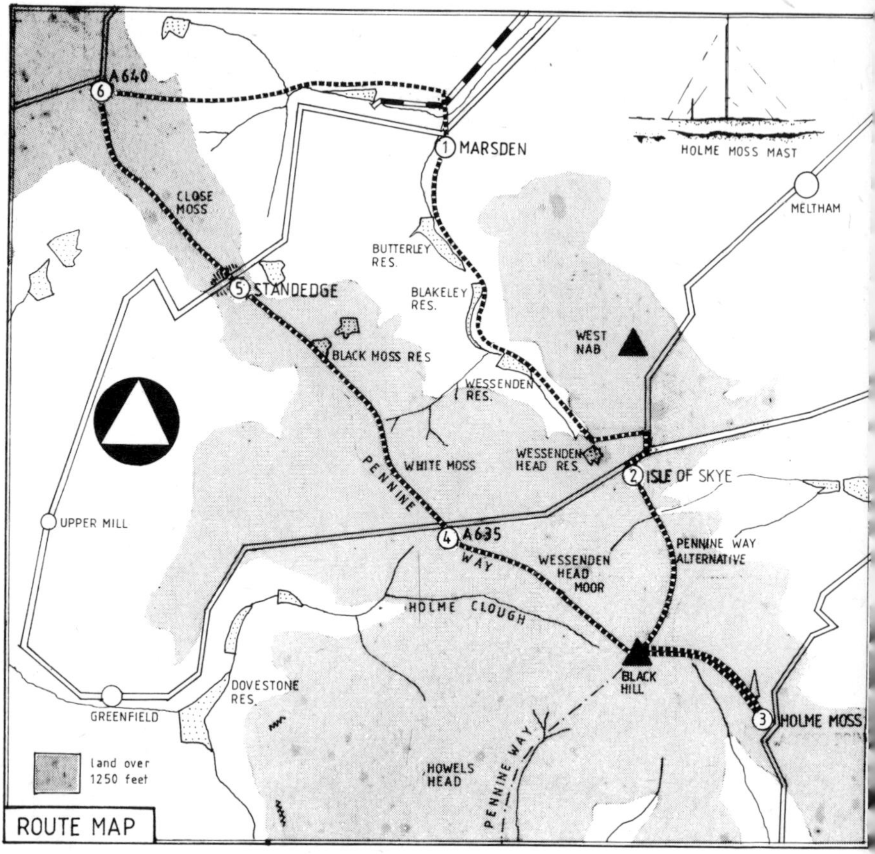

ROUTE MAP
A640
6
CLOSE MOSS
5 STANDEDGE
1 MARSDEN
HOLME MOSS MAST
MELTHAM
BUTTERLEY RES.
BLAKELEY RES.
WEST NAB
BLACK MOSS RES
WESSENDEN RES.
WESSENDEN HEAD RES.
2 ISLE OF SKYE
PENNINE WAY
WHITE MOSS
UPPER MILL
4 A635
PENNINE WAY ALTERNATIVE
WESSENDEN HEAD MOOR
HOLME CLOUGH
BLACK HILL
3 HOLME MOSS
GREENFIELD
DOVESTONE RES.
HOWELS HEAD
land over 1250 feet

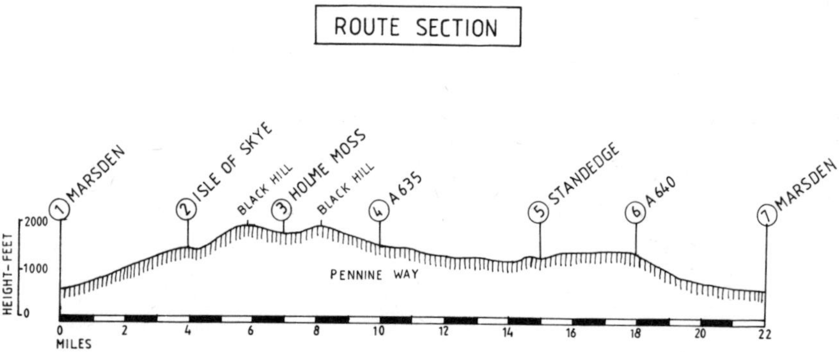

ROUTE SECTION
1 MARSDEN
2 ISLE OF SKYE
BLACK HILL
3 HOLME MOSS
BLACK HILL
4 A635
5 STANDEDGE
6 A640
7 MARSDEN
HEIGHT-FEET
2000
1000
0
PENNINE WAY
0 2 4 6 8 10 12 14 16 18 20 22
MILES

Saddleworth Five Trig Points Walk

Start and Finish — Greenfield
Clarence Hotel
Distance — 20 miles (32 km)
Ascent — 3100 feet (345m)
Time Limit — None
Maps — O.S. Peak District Tourist
(one inch)
Origin — Bob Tait, 1971

Introduction: There can be little doubt that the moorland wilderness of the High Peak has a strange fascination. Since 1971 when this route was devised as an exercise for the Oldham Mountain Rescue Team it has become something of a modern day classic. A high level circuit that can be guaranteed to provide a tough but rewarding test of navigation and stamina, particularly when it is wet and misty!

Completions: Total number of recorded completions — 980. Fastest recorded completion — 2 hours 38 minutes by Messrs Robinson and Monk.

Further Information: Send a large stamped addressed envelope for details of the route, badge and certificate to Bob Tait, 6 Leefields Close, Uppermill, Oldham, Lancs OL3 6HF.

Reference: *Walks around Saddleworth,* Bob Tait, 1979. Published privately and available from Bob Tait at the above address.

Route Outline and Log:

No	Grid Ref	Location	Height Feet	Distance mls	km	2½ mph pace	Date
1	002 040	Greenfield	550	0	0	0	....
2	003 028	Alphin Pike	1537	1	2	0.25	....
3	046 012	Featherbed Moss	1774	4	6	1.35	....
4	078 047	Black Hill	1908	8	13	3.10	....
5	076 088	West Neb	1641	12	19	4.50	....
6	057 086	Wessenden Res	1000	14	22	5.35	....
7	021 069	Broadstone Hill	1491	17	27	6.50	....
8	010 051	Pots and Pans	1350	19	30	7.35	....
9	002 040	Greenfield	550	20	32	8.00	....
						Total time	....

SADDLEWORTH FIVE TRIG POINTS WALK

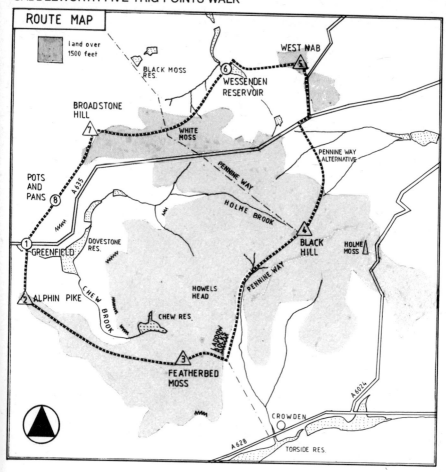

ROUTE MAP

land over 1500 feet

BLACK MOSS RES.

WEST NAB

6 WESSENDEN RESERVOIR

5

BROADSTONE HILL

7

WHITE MOSS

PENNINE WAY ALTERNATIVE

POTS AND PANS

8

A 635

PENNINE WAY

HOLME BROOK

BLACK HILL

4

HOLME MOSS

1 GREENFIELD

DOVESTONE RES.

PENNINE WAY

CHEW BROOK

HOWELS HEAD

2 ALPHIN PIKE

CHEW RES.

LADDOW ROCKS

3

FEATHERBED MOSS

CROWDEN

A 6024

A 628

TORSIDE RES.

ROUTE SECTION

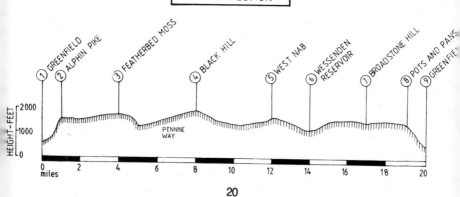

① GREENFIELD
② ALPHIN PIKE
③ FEATHERBED MOSS
④ BLACK HILL
⑤ WEST NAB
⑥ WESSENDEN RESERVOIR
⑦ BROADSTONE HILL
⑧ POTS AND PANS
⑨ GREENFIELD

HEIGHT – FEET

2000
1000
0

PENNINE WAY

0 2 4 6 8 10 12 14 16 18 20
miles

20

Ten Reservoirs Walk

Start and Finish — Dovestone Reservoir Car Park, Near Greenfield.
Distance — 22 miles (35 km)
Ascent — 3750 feet (1143 m)
Time Limit — None
Maps — O.S. Peak District Tourist (one inch)
Origin — Bob Tait, 1973

Introduction: A companion walk to the Five Trigs, this is another demanding but worthwhile walk encircling the high featureless country of the Saddleworth Moors. Again it is a walk to be undertaken only by capable well equipped walkers skilled with map and compass.

Completions: Total number of recorded completions — 607. Record times are not yet maintained due to the nature of the route.

Further Information: Send a large stamped addressed envelope for details of the route, badge and certificate to Bob Tait, 6 Leefields Close, Uppermill, Oldham, Lancs OL3 6HF.

Reference: *Walks around Saddleworth,* Bob Tait, 1979. Published privately and available from Bob Tait at the above address.

Route Outline and Log:

No	Grid Ref	Location	Height Feet	Distance mls	km	2½ mph pace	Date
1	014 034	Dovestone Res	700	0	0	0	....
2	020 046	Yeoman Hey Res	800	1	2	0.25	....
3	027 055	Greenfield Res	950	2	3	0.50	....
4	033 086	Black Moss Res	1350	6	9	2.25	....
5	038 089	Swellands Res	1300	6½	10	2.35	....
6	054 097	Blakeley Res	900	7½	12	3.00	....
7	058 088	Wessenden Res	1000	8½	14	3.25	....
8	070 077	Wessenden Head Res	1250	10	16	4.00	....
9	073 993	Torside Res	700	16	25	6.25	....
10	035 018	Chew Res	1600	20	32	8.00	....
11	014 034	Dovestone Res	700	22	35	8.50	....
						Total time	....

TEN RESERVOIRS WALK

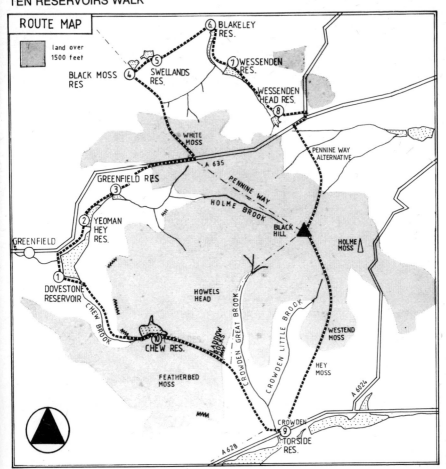

ROUTE MAP

land over 1500 feet

BLACK MOSS RES

SWELLANDS RES.

BLACKELEY RES.

WESSENDEN RES.

WESSENDEN HEAD RES.

WHITE MOSS

A 635

PENNINE WAY ALTERNATIVE

GREENFIELD RES

PENNINE WAY

HOLME BROOK

YEOMAN HEY RES.

GREENFIELD

BLACK HILL

HOLME MOSS

DOVESTONE RESERVOIR

CHEW BROOK

HOWELS HEAD

CROWDEN GREAT BROOK

CROWDEN LITTLE BROOK

WESTEND MOSS

CHEW RES.

HARROW ROCKS

HEY MOSS

A 6024

FEATHERBED MOSS

CROWDEN

TORSIDE RES.

A 628

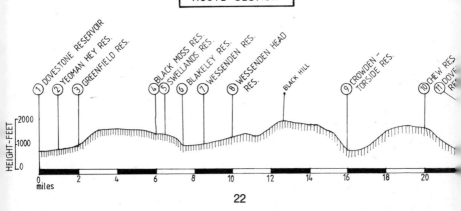

ROUTE SECTION

① DOVESTONE RESERVOIR
② YEOMAN HEY RES.
③ GREENFIELD RES.
④ BLACK MOSS RES.
⑤ SWELLANDS RES.
⑥ BLACKELEY RES.
⑦ WESSENDEN RES.
⑧ WESSENDEN HEAD RES.
BLACK HILL
⑨ CROWDEN – TORSIDE RES.
⑩ CHEW RES.
⑪ DOVE RES.

HEIGHT–FEET

2000

0

miles 0   2   4   6   8   10   12   14   16   18   20

22

Limey Way

Start — Castleton
Finish — Thorpe
Distance — 38 miles (61 km)
Ascent — 3000 feet (914 m)
Time Limit — 24 hours (optional)
Maps — O.S. Peak District Tourist (one inch)
O.S. Sheets 110, 119 (1:50,000)
O.S. White Peak Outdoor Leisure Map (1:25,000)
Origin — John Merrill, 1969

Introduction: With a list of relentless achievements to his name, John Merrill is possibly Britain's best known walker. One of his most notable walks is the 7000 mile British Coastal Walk completed in 1978. As a local to the Peak District, John inaugurated the Limey Way in 1969. The objective of the route is a north-south traverse of the White Peak limestone country along a chain of no less than 18 varied and picturesque dales. The route can be done as a continuous walk within 24 hours, while Monyash provides a convenient overnight stop for those wishing to take longer. A badge is available for successful completions.

Completions: No information available.

Reference: *The Limey Way*, John N. Merrill (Dalesman, 1979).

Route Outline and Log:

No	Grid Ref	Location	Height Feet	Distance mls	km	2½ mph pace	Date . . . .
1	151 830	Castleton	600	0	0	0	. . . .
2	115 791	Peak Forest	1000	4	6	1.35	. . . .
3	141 734	Millers Dale	750	8	13	3.20	. . . .
4	151 665	Monyash	850	16	25	6.25	. . . .
5	220 646	Alport	450	21	34	8.25	. . . .
6	155 594	Biggin	950	30	48	12.00	. . . .
7	157 504	Thorpe	600	38	61	15.10	. . . .
						Total time	. . . .

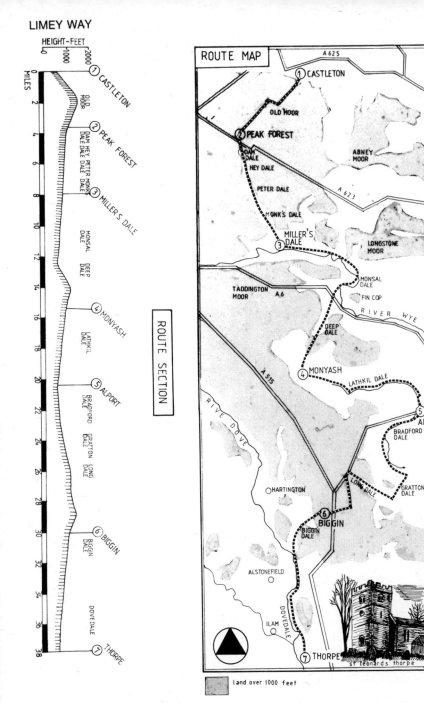

LIMEY WAY

HEIGHT—FEET

ROUTE SECTION

ROUTE MAP

A 625

① CASTLETON

OLD MOOR

② PEAK FOREST

DAM DALE
HEY DALE

ABNEY MOOR

A 623

PETER DALE

MONK'S DALE

③ MILLER'S DALE

LONGSTONE MOOR

MONSAL DALE

TADDINGTON MOOR

A 6

FIN COP

RIVER WYE

DEEP DALE

④ MONYASH

LATHKIL DALE

A 515

⑤ ALPORT

BRADFORD DALE

RIVER DOVE

LONG DALE

GRATTON DALE

HARTINGTON

⑥ BIGGIN

BIGGIN DALE

ALSTONEFIELD

DOVEDALE

ILAM

⑦ THORPE

st leonards thorpe

land over 1000 feet

24

Cal-Der-Went Walk

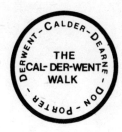

Start — Horbury Bridge
Finish — Snake Road, Ladybower
Distance — 29 miles (46 km)
Ascent — 2750 feet (838 m)
Time Limit — None
Maps — O.S. sheet 110 (1:50,000)
Origin — St John's Methodist Church, Ossett, 1978.

Introduction: The inaugural walk by the Ossett St. John's Methodist Church Lyke Wake Club took place in 1978. Dalesman published the guide in 1979. This is a pleasant walk from the River Calder in West Yorkshire to the River Derwent in North Derbyshire contrasting rural scenery with the wild moorland landscape of the Peak. The walk may be done in either direction, as a continuous exercise or in sections to suit your convenience.

Completions: Total number of recorded completions — 1226. Fastest recorded completion — 4 hours 55 minutes by G. Hulley.

Further Information: Full route details are contained in the guidebook below. Details of badges and cerfificates can be obtained by sending a stamped addressed envelope to The Cal-Der-Went Walk Recorder, Fern Cottage, Cardigan Lane, Manor Road, Ossett, West Yorkshire WF5 0LT.

Reference: *The Cal-Der-Went Walk,* Geoffrey Carr (Dalesman 1979).

Route Outline and Log:

No	Grid Ref	Location	Height	Distance mls	km	2½ mph pace	Date ....
1	280 179	Horbury Bridge	100	0	0	0	....
2	281 125	Bretton Park	300	5	8	2.00	....
3	283 084	Cawthorne	300	9	14	3.35	....
4	245 035	Penistone	650	13	21	5.10	....
5	203 009	Langsett	1000	17	27	6.50	....
6	169 952	Slippery Stones	950	22	35	8.50	....
7	197 864	Snake Road	750	29	46	11.35	....

						Total time	....

CAL-DER-WENT WALK

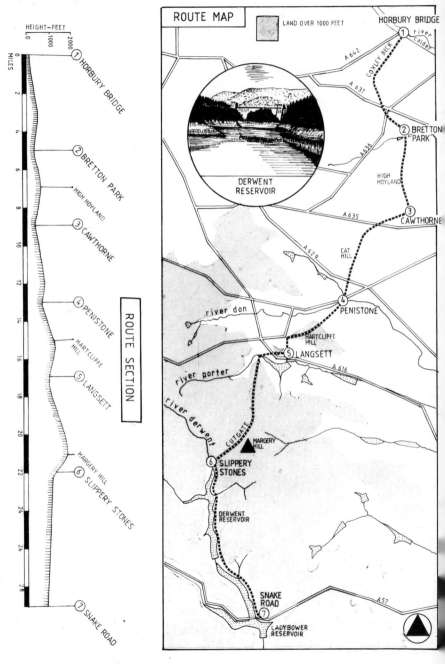

ROUTE MAP

LAND OVER 1000 FEET

HORBURY BRIDGE

① HORBURY BRIDGE
river calder
A 642
COXLEY BECK
A 637
② BRETTON PARK
A 636
HIGH HOYLAND
A 635
③ CAWTHORNE
A 629
CAT HILL
④ PENISTONE
river don
HARTCLIFFE HILL
⑤ LANGSETT
A 616
river porter
river derwent
CUTGATE
MARGERY HILL
⑥ SLIPPERY STONES
DERWENT RESERVOIR
SNAKE ROAD
⑦
LADYBOWER RESERVOIR
A 57

DERWENT RESERVOIR

HEIGHT—FEET
0   1000   2000
0
MILES

ROUTE SECTION

① HORBURY BRIDGE
② BRETTON PARK
HIGH HOYLAND
③ CAWTHORNE
④ PENISTONE
HARTCLIFFE HILL
⑤ LANGSETT
MARGERY HILL
⑥ SLIPPERY STONES
⑦ SNAKE ROAD

Peakland Heritage Walk

Start and Finish — Hathersage
Distance — 36 miles (58 km)
Ascent — 4000 feet (1220 m)
Time Limit — 15 hours (optional)
Maps — O.S. Peak District Tourist
(one inch)
O.S. sheets 110, 119
(1:50,000)
Origin — T. Wimbush, 1975

Introduction: This was conceived initially as a training route for the 1975 Downsman Hundred event organised by the Long Distance Walker's Association. The route was then promoted by Battyeford Scout Group as a challenge walk in 1980.

The attractive circuit combines and contrasts the limestone dales of the White Peak with the high gritstone edges of the east taking in a variety of features including Lathkill Dale National Nature Reserve, Padley Gorge, historic Bakewell and Hathersage, relics of the industrial revolution, ancient hillforts and the majestic Chatsworth. The walk may be undertaken within a 15 hour time limit or over a longer period.

Completions: Total number of recorded completions — 803. Fastest recorded completion — 4 hours 58 minutes by M. Hartley.

Further Information: For a leaflet containing a detailed route description and information on the badge and certificate send a large stamped addressed envelope to Mrs M. Hickling, Battyeford Scout Group, School House, Stocksbank Road, Mirfield, West Yorkshire WF14 9QT.

Route Outline and Log:

No	Grid Ref	Location	Height Feet	Distance mls	km	2½ mph pace	Date
1	230 815	Hathersage	500	0	0	0	....
2	178 778	Great Hucklow	1000	6	10	2.25	....
3	151 665	Monyash	850	15	24	6.00	....
4	220 687	Bakewell	400	21	34	8.25	....
5	258 722	Nether End	350	25	40	10.00	....
6	251 786	Grindleford Stn	500	30	48	12.00	....
7	230 815	Hathersage	500	36	58	14.25	....
						Total time	....

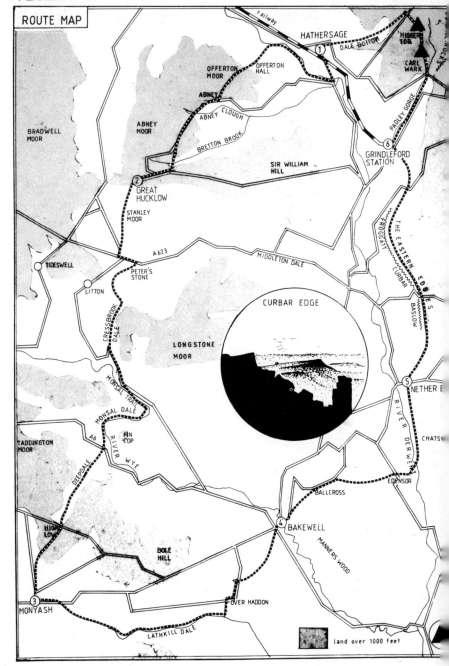

ROUTE MAP

HATHERSAGE

OFFERTON MOOR
OFFERTON HALL
ABNEY
ABNEY CLOUGH
ABNEY MOOR
BRETTON BROOK
BRADWELL MOOR
SIR WILLIAM HILL

GREAT HUCKLOW
STANLEY MOOR

TIDESWELL
A 623
MIDDLETON DALE

PETER'S STONE
LITTON

CURBAR EDGE

CRESSBROOK DALE

LONGSTONE MOOR

MONSAL TRAIL
MONSAL DALE
PIN COP
A6
TADDINGTON MOOR
RIVER WYE
DEEPDALE

HIGH LOW
BOLE HILL

MONYASH
OVER HADDON
LATHKILL DALE

GRINDLEFORD STATION

PADLEY GORGE

HIGGER TOR
CARL WARK

THE EASTERN EDGES
FROGGATT
CURBAR
BASLOW

NETHER E

RIVER DERWENT
CHATSW

EDENSOR
BALLCROSS
BAKEWELL
MANNERS WOOD

land over 1000 feet

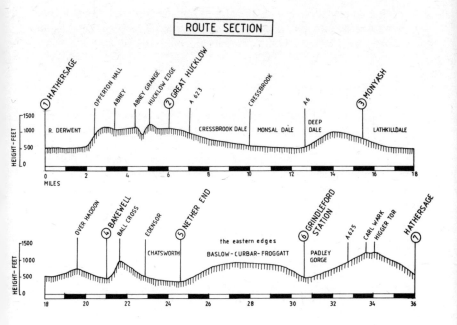

Leek Moors 14-400's

Start and Finish — Flash
Distance — 36 miles (58 km)   **Ascent — 4500 feet (1372 m)**
Time Limit — None
Maps — O.S. sheets 118, 119 (1:50,000)
        The White Peak Outdoor Leisure Map (1:25,000)
Origin — Staffordshire LDWA. 1981.

Introduction: The Staffordshire LDWA originated this challenge in the south-west corner of the Peak in 1981. Flash which claims the highest village inn in the Kingdom provides the base for this route, which as well as taking in the high gritstone area of north-east Staffordshire also links the secluded valley of the Manifold, Hamps, Churnet and Dane. Certificates are available for successful completions.

Completions: Total number of completions — 7. Fastest recorded completion — 11 hours 36 minutes by N. Mitton.

29

Further Information: For details of the route description and certificate send a large stamped addressed envelope to:- The Chairman, Staffs LDWA, 32 Manifold Road, Forsbrook, near Blythe Bridge, North Staffordshire ST11 9BN

Here are also vast Rocks which suprise with Admiration called the Henclouds and Leek Roches. They are of so great a Height and afford such stupendous Prospects that one could hardly believe they were anywhere to be found but in Picture.

'The Complete History of Staffordshire' (1730)

Route Outline and Log:

No	Grid Ref	Location	Height Meters	Distance mls	Distance km	2½ mph pace	Date . . . .
1	025 672	Flash	457	0	0	0	. . . .
2	055 658	Hollingsclough Moor	424	3	5	1.10	. . . .
3	054 624	Round Knowle	435	7	11	2.50	. . . .
4	077 599	Revidge	402	10	16	4.00	. . . .
5	052 585	Royledge	425	12	19	4.50	. . . .
6	038 575	Mixon Hill	424	14	22	5.35	. . . .
7	038 543	Moorside	405	17	27	6.50	. . . .
8	029 553	Moor Top	400	18	29	7.10	. . . .
9	041 610	Merryton Low	489	22	35	8.50	. . . .
10	004 627	Summerhill	472	25	40	10.00	. . . .
11	002 639	Roach Summit	505	26	42	10.25	. . . .
12	995 644	Roach End	403	27	44	10.50	. . . .
13	009 673	Turn Edge	433	32	51	12.50	. . . .
14	026 690	Drystone Edge	488	34	54	13.35	. . . .
15	027 675	Oliver Hill	513	35	56	14.00	. . . .
16	025 672	Flash	457	36	58	14.25	. . . .

Total time . . . .

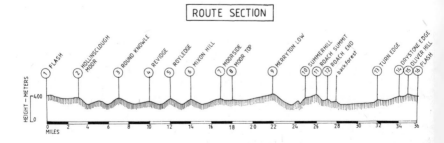

ROUTE SECTION

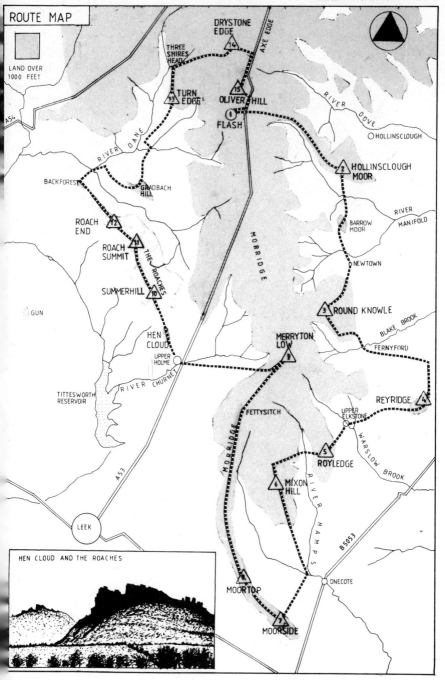

ROUTE MAP

LAND OVER
1000 FEET

DRYSTONE EDGE
14

AXE EDGE

THREE SHIRES HEAD

TURN EDGE
13

OLIVER HILL
15

FLASH
1

RIVER DOVE

HOLLINSCLOUGH

HOLLINSCLOUGH MOOR
2

RIVER DANE

BACKFOREST

GRADBACH HILL

ROACH END
12

ROACH SUMMIT
11

THE ROACHES

SUMMERHILL
10

HEN CLOUD

UPPER HOLME

GUN

MORRIDGE

BARROW MOOR

RIVER MANIFOLD

NEWTOWN

ROUND KNOWLE
3

BLAKE BROOK

FERNYFORD

MERRYTON LOW
9

REYRIDGE
4

UPPER ELKSTONE

WARSLOW BROOK

RIVER CHURNET

TITTESWORTH RESERVOIR

FETTYSITCH

MORRIDGE

ROYLEDGE
5

MIXON HILL
6

RIVER HAMPS

A53

LEEK

B5053

ONECOTE

MOORTOP
8

MOORSIDE
7

HEN CLOUD AND THE ROACHES

New Five Trig Points Walk

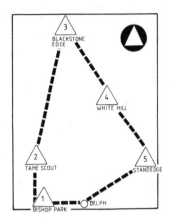

Start and Finish — Swan Inn, Delph (Grid Ref. 985 079)
Distance — 18 miles (29 km)
Time Limit — None
Maps — O.S. sheets 109, 110 (1:50,000)
Origin — Bob Tait, 1980

Description: This is the third of Bob Tait's outings in the Saddleworth area. The easier terrain provides a contrast to its companion walks although a height of over 1500 feet is still reached. At only eighteen miles the walk does not make the long distance qualification but does complete this Saddleworth trio of walks. An attractive badge and cerfificate is available for successful completions.

Route Outline: Swan Inn, Delph — GR 985 079, Bishop Park trig. point — GR 968 081, Tame Scout trig. point — GR 961 105, M62 bridge — GR 953 142, Lydgate — GR 955 165, Blackstone Edge trig. point — GR 972 164, White Hill trig. point — GR 991 132, Standedge trig. point- GR 012 014, Lark Hill — GR 994 075, Swan Inn Delph.

Completions: Total number of recorded completions to date — 399. Fastest recorded completion 2 hours 44 minutes by Bob Tait.

Further Information: Send a large stamped addressed envelope (9″ × 5″) for an information sheet containing details of the route, badge and certificate to the following address: Mr R. Tait, 6 Leefields Close, Uppermill, Oldham, Greater Manchester, OL3 6LA.

Ancient Relics, Ruins and Old Legends of the Saddleworth Moor

Start and Finish — Binn Green Picnic Site (Grid Ref 018 044)
Distance — 20 — 25 miles (optional)   **Time Limit — None**
Map — O.S. sheet 110 (1:50,000)   **Origin — Bob Tait, 1982**

Description: The theme of this outing is the exploration of the local history of the area, from shooting cabins and air crash sites to the scene of the macabre 1965 Moors Murders. No badge or certificate are awarded for the walk but completions are recorded. Bob Tait comments that any connection between the inaugurators and the title of the walk is entirely intentional!

Route Outline: Binn Green Picnic Site — GR 018 044, Ashway Gap — GR 022 042, Wimberry Rocks — GR 014 025, Swineshaw Reservoir — GR 006 995, Laddow Rocks — GR 057 015, Crowden Little Brook GR 075 023, Hollin Brown Knoll — GR 036 064, Broadstone Hill — GR 021 069, Alderman Hill — GR 015 046, Binn Green Picnic Site.

Further Information: Send a large stamped addressed envelope (9″ × 5″) for an information sheet containing details of the route to the following address: Mr R. Tait, 6 Leefields Close, Uppermill, Oldham, Greater Manchester OL3 6LA.

Cuckoo Walk

Start and Finish — Marsden (Grid Ref 048 115)
Distance — 20 Miles (32 km)
Time Limit — 10 hours
Map — O.S. Sheet 110 (1:50,000)
Origin — Marsden Scout Group, 1976

Description: The Cuckoo Walk takes its name from the Marsden Cuckoo Legend which held that to capture the Cuckoo was also to capture spring and summer, and Marsden would become a 'charming place to live'. The Cuckoo and Bog Dodgers coincide with each other for the most part. Badge collectors may speculate that if they make some minor deviations would they be able to purchase two different badges for completing what is essentially the same route!

Completions: Total recorded completions — 1160. Fastest recorded completion — 2 hours 30 minutes by R. Tait.

Route Outline: Marsden — Wessenden Reservoir — West Nab — Black Hill — Dean Head Hill — A635 — Standedge — A640 — Marsden.

Further Information: Send a large stamped addressed envelope to Mr. D. E. Wilkins, Scout Leader, 22 Lane Ings, Marsden, Huddersfield, HD7 6JP.

Classic Walks

The Big Walks and the companion volume *Classic Walks* represent perhaps the most inspiring and exhilarating collection of photographs and walks on the British mountains ever to be compiled. Fifty-five routes are included in *The Big Walks,* ten of which are in England and two of which fall within the Peak, the Marsden — Edale and the Derwent Watershed referred to elsewhere (see pages 8 and 10). *Classic Walks* contains seventy-nine routes, thirty-two of which are in England with four in the Peak District, as listed below.

The Eastern Edge of the Peak — Classic Walk 41
The Round of Kinder Scout from Edale — Classic Walk 42
Dovedale from Axe Edge — Classic Walk 47
The Western Peak by the Gritstone Trail — Classic Walk 43

Reference: *Classic Walks,* K. Wilson and R. Gilbert (Diadem, 1982).

Gritstone Edge Walk

Start — Derwent Reservoir (Grid Ref. 172 921)
Finish — Baslow (Grid Ref 253 724)
Distance — 23 miles (37 km)
Time Limit — None
Maps — O.S. Peak District Tourist (one inch), O.S. sheets 110, 119
      (1:50,000)
Origin — John N. Merrill, 1969

Description: A route along the eastern edges of the Peak taking in Derwent, Stanage, Burbage, Froggatt, Curbar, Baslow, Gardoms, Birchen and Chatsworth edges.

Reference: *Walking in Derbyshire* John N. Merrill (Dalesman 1969); *Peak District Marathons,* John N. Merrill (JNM Publications, 1982).

Trail Blazer Challenge Walk

Start and Finish — Bakewell (Grid Ref 217 684)
Distance — 25 miles (40 km)
Map — O.S. Peak District Tourist (one inch)
Origin — John N. Merrill 1982

Description: A new route round the White Peak including Ballcross, Rowsley, Stanton Moor, Birchover, Robin Hood's stride, Youlgreave, Cales Dale, Monyash, Flagg, Taddington, Monsal Dale and Great Longstone.

Reference: *Trail-Blazer Challenge Walk,* J. N. Merrill, (J. N. M. Publications, 1983).

Three Feathers Walks

Third Feather — Start and Finish — Yorkshire Bridge Inn (Grid Ref. 201 850)
Distance — 26 miles (42 km)
Time Limit — NoneMap — O.S. Peak District Tourist (one inch)
Origin — The Bard of Barking Walking Club, 1983

Description: One of the most recent additions to the walking scene this breaks new ground by requiring the completion of three walks each within a different National Park. All the walks must be completed within the twelve month period between January 1 and December 31. The first feather is a 30 mile circuit of the Yorkshire Dales based on Kettlewell, the second a 30 mile circuit of the North York Moors from the White Horse Kilburn and the third feather this walk in the Peak District.

Route Outline: Yorkshire Bridge Inn — Win Hill — Lose Hill — Mam Tor — Lords seat — Brown Knoll — Kinder Low — Kinder Downfall — Ashop Head — Ashop Clough — Snake Inn — Hayridge Farm — Crookstone Barn — Wooler Knoll — Yorkshire Bridge Inn.

Further Information: Send a large stamped addressed envelope to: The 'Bards Recorder', Keith Brown, Dale House, 35 Bawtry Road, Listerdale, Rotherham S66 0AR.

Challenge Events
and Fell Races

KINDERLOW END (J. ALLEN)

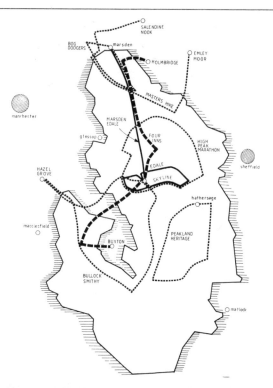

High Peak Marathon	41 miles	(66 km)
Bullock Smithy Hike	56 miles	(90 km)
Four Inns Walk	43 miles	(69 km)
Masters Hike	40 miles	(64 km)
Edale Skyline Fell Race	22 miles	(35 km)
Marsden-Edale Trog	19 miles	(31 km)
Bog Dodgers Event	22 miles	(35 km)
Wild Ways Walk	20 miles	(32 km)
YHA Peak Marathons	Various	
Rotherham Round Walk	25 miles	(40 km)
Peakland Heritage Event	36 miles	(58 km)
Peakland Hundred	100 miles	(161 km)
Bolsover District Walk	Various	
Boscobel Walk	Various	

High Peak Marathon

Start and Finish — Edale Village Hall
Distance — 41 miles (66 km)
Time Limit — Restricted by Checkpoint closures
Maps — O.S. Peak District Tourist (one inch)
       Dark Peak Outdoor Leisure Map (1:25,000)
Organiser — Sheffield University Youth Hostels Society
Current Date — February/March

Introduction: The route is based upon the Derwent Watershed Walk inaugurated by the legendary Eustace Thomas of the RucksackClub in 1918 (see page 10). Sheffield University Youth Hostels Society launched the event in 1972 spearheaded by Haydn Morris.

This is a tough winter marathon for teams of four. Even the country's top long distance fell runners hesitate before entering this one! Success has eluded many teams with the completion rate rarely rising above the 50 per cent level.

Course Record: 10 hours 10 minutes by the Rucksack Club.

Further Information: Send a large stamped addressed envelope for details of the next event (after November) to Harvard Prosser, 94 Green Drift, Royston, Herts 5G8 5BT.

ute Outline and Log:

⟩	Grid Ref	Checkpoint	Height Feet	Distance mls	km	2½ mph Pace	Date ....
▮	123 853	Edale V. Hall	750	0	0	0	....
▮	135 845	Hollins Cross	1300	1	2	0.25	....
▮	153 853	Lose Hill	1550	2	3	0.50	....
▮	187 851	Win Hill	1500	5	8	2.00	....
▮	227 853	High Neb	1450	8½	14	3.25	....
▮	231 878	Moscar	1200	10½	17	4.10	....
▮	202 880	Derwent Edge	1450	12½	20	5.00	....
▮	206 934	Bradfield Path	1550	16	26	6.25	....
▮	185 960	Cut Gate	1700	18½	30	7.25	....
▮	177 969	Outer Edge	1800	19½	32	7.50	....
▮	132 963	Swains Head	1600	23	37	9.10	....
▮	115 963	Bleaklow Stones	2050	25	40	10.00	....
▮	092 958	Bleaklow Head	2050	26½	47	10.35	....
▮	088 929	Snake Road	1700	29½	47	11.50	....
▮	062 904	Mill Hill	1750	31	50	12.25	....
▮	081 861	Edale Cross	1750	34½	56	13.50	....
▮	112 835	Rushup Edge	1800	38	61	15.10	....
▮	135 845	Hollins Cross	1300	40	65	16.00	....
▮	123 853	Edale V. Hall	750	41	66	16.25	....

| | | | | | Total time | .... |

HIGH PEAK MARATHON

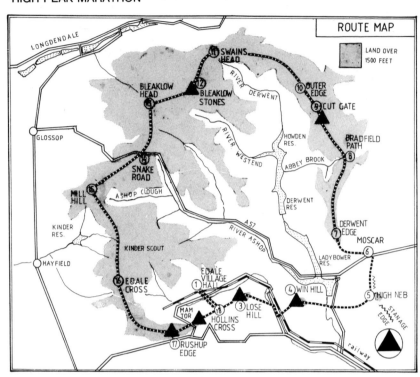

ROUTE MAP

LAND OVER 1500 FEET

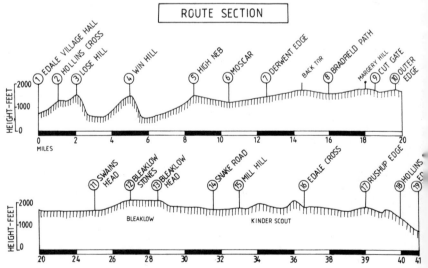

ROUTE SECTION

40

Bullock Smithy Hike

Start and Finish — Hazel Grove
Distance — 56 miles (90 km)
Ascent — 6000 feet (1846 m)
Time Limit — 24 hours
Maps — O.S. Peak District Tourist (one inch)
Organiser — 3rd Hazel Grove Scout Group
Date — September, 1st weekend.

Introduction: Bullock Smithy is the former name of Hazel Grove and was officially changed in 1835. The event, first organised in 1976, is open to both members of the Scout movement and the general public. This attractive circuit round the western and central Peak has established it as one of the most popular events on the calendar. A good selection of trophies is available for individuals and teams with the Bullock Smithy Trophy going to the fastest individual. Badges and certificates are available to all successful participants.

Course Record: 8 hours 48 minutes by S. Parr.

Further Information: Send a large stamped addressed envelope after December for entry form and details to Fielding Lord, 89 Bramhall Moor Lane, Hazel Grove, Stockport.

ute Outline and Log:

o	Grid Ref	Checkpoint	Height Feet	Distance mls	km	2½ mph pace	Date ....
1	925 862	Hazel Grove	280	0	0	0	....
2	974 813	Bow Stones	1300	5	8	2	....
3	037 844	Chinley Church	1400	10	16	4	....
4	079 861	Edale Cross	1800	14	22	5.35	....
5	124 853	Edale	770	18	29	7.10	....
6	149 830	Castleton	600	20	32	8	....
7	115 792	Peak Forest	1200	24	39	9.35	....
8	142 735	Millers Dale	850	28	45	11.10	....
9	118 692	Chelmorton	1270	32	51	12.50	....
0	091 669	Earl Sterndale	1040	35	56	14	....
1	034 698	Axe Edge	1600	40	64	16	....
2	999 722	Cat and Fiddle	1690	43	69	17.10	....
3	994 767	Pyms Chair	1500	46	74	18.25	....
4	981 821	Cocks Knoll	1000	51	82	20.25	....
5	925 862	Hazel Grove	280	56	90	22.25	....

| | | | | | | Total time | .... |

BULLOCK SMITHY HIKE

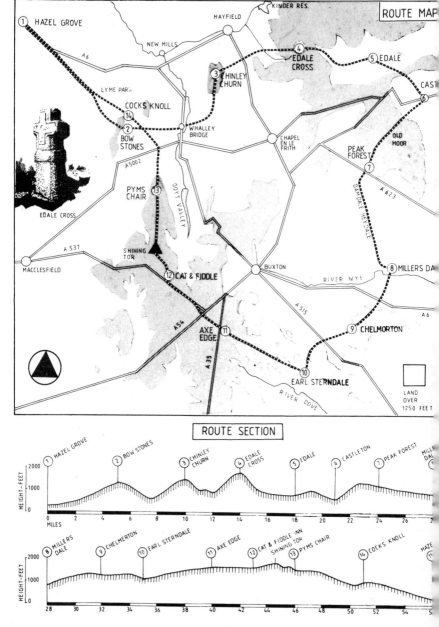

Four Inns Walk (Scout Event)

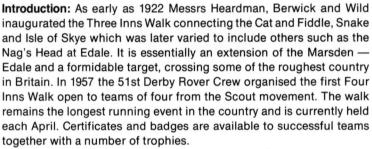

Start — Holmbridge
Finish — Buxton
Distance — 43 miles (69 km)
Ascent — 7000 feet (2154 m)
Time Limit — Restricted by checkpoint closures
Map — O.S. Peak District Tourist (one inch)
Organiser: 51st Derby Rover Crew
Current date: April

Introduction: As early as 1922 Messrs Heardman, Berwick and Wild inaugurated the Three Inns Walk connecting the Cat and Fiddle, Snake and Isle of Skye which was later varied to include others such as the Nag's Head at Edale. It is essentially an extension of the Marsden — Edale and a formidable target, crossing some of the roughest country in Britain. In 1957 the 51st Derby Rover Crew organised the first Four Inns Walk open to teams of four from the Scout movement. The walk remains the longest running event in the country and is currently held each April. Certificates and badges are available to successful teams together with a number of trophies.

Cours Record: Fastest time — 8 hours 29 minutes by Viking VSU 'A'.

Further Information: Send a large stamped addressed envelope to: T. P. Rogers, 'Penylan' Monyash Road, Bakewell, Derbyshire.

Reference: *The Four Inns Story,* C. Manning. Available from the above address.

ute Outline and Log:

Grid Ref	Checkpoint	Height Feet	Distance mls	km	2½ mph Pace	Date ....
121 068	Holmbridge	700	0	0	0	....
077 073	Isle of Skye	1450	3½	6	1.25	....
079 001	Hey Moss	1372	9	14	3.35	....
074 993	Crowden	650	10	16	4.00	....
058 980	Torside	700	12	19	4.50	....
096 929	Doctors Gate	1500	18	29	7.10	....
112 906	Snake Inn	1050	20	32	8.00	....
124 853	Edale	750	24	39	9.35	....
054 806	Chapel	800	30	48	12.00	....
032 765	White Hall	1300	34	55	13.35	....
001 719	Cat And Fiddle	1690	38	61	15.10	....
067 710	Buxton	1200	43	69	17.10	....
					Total time	....

FOUR INNS WALK

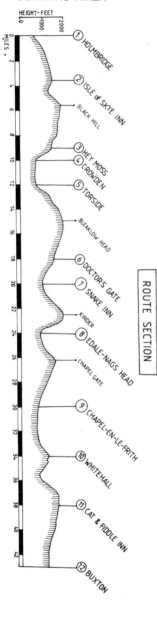

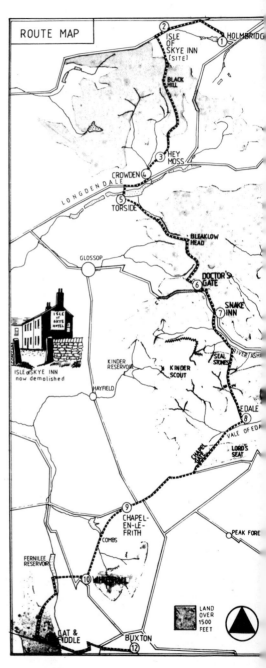

Masters Hike (Scout Event)

Start — Salendine Nook
Finish — Emley Moor
Distance — 40 miles (64 km)
Ascent — 3300 feet (1015 m)
Time Limit — Restricted by Checkpoint closures
Maps — O.S. sheet 110 (1:50,000)
Organiser — Holme Valley District Scout Fellowship
Current date — November

Introduction: Originated in 1969 the Masters Hike provides a tough test round the wild moorland country of the Peak District National Park and South Pennines. The hike is open to teams of four who must be members of the Scout and Guide Movement. Badges and certificates are available to successful participants together with numerous trophies.

Course Record: 9 hours 38 minutes by 68th Doncaster Venture Scout Unit.

Further Information: Send a large stamped addressed envelope to Doug Farrow, 71 Charlecote Road, Poynton, Cheshire, SK12 1DJ.

Route Outline and Log:

No	Grid Ref	Checkpoint	Height	Distance mls	km	2½ mph pace	Date ....
1	109 175	Salendine Nook	800	0	0	0	....
2	047 138	Bradshaw	900	5	8	2.00	....
3	032 104	Pule Hill	1400	9	15	3.35	....
4	054 063	White Moss	1615	12	19	4.50	....
5	098 038	Holme Moss	1700	16	25	6.25	....
6	106 026	Britland Edge	1717	17	27	6.50	....
7	118 030	Withens Edge	1600	18	29	7.10	....
8	140 007	Saltersbrook	1250	20	32	8.00	....
9	132 982	Swains Head	1650	21	34	8.25	....
10	170 953	Slippery Stones	1000	25	40	10.00	....
11	198 007	Cut Gate	850	30	48	12.00	....
12	194 035	Hazlehead	900	32	51	12.50	....
13	198 069	Broadstone Lodge	1000	35	56	14.00	....
14	208 097	Shelley	700	38	61	15.00	....
15	220 130	Emley Moor	850	40	64	16.00	....

Total time ....

MASTERS HIKE

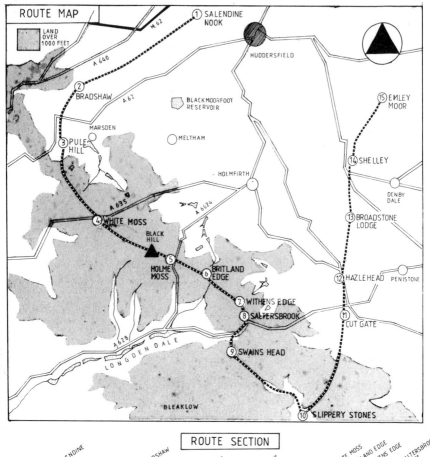

ROUTE MAP

LAND OVER 1000 FEET

① SALENDINE NOOK
② BRADSHAW
③ PULE HILL
④ WHITE MOSS
⑤ HOLME MOSS
⑥ BRITLAND EDGE
⑦ WITHENS EDGE
⑧ SALTERSBROOK
⑨ SWAINS HEAD
⑩ SLIPPERY STONES
⑪ CUT GATE
⑫ HAZLEHEAD
⑬ BROADSTONE LODGE
⑭ SHELLEY
⑮ EMLEY MOOR

HUDDERSFIELD
BLACKMOORFOOT RESERVOIR
MARSDEN
MELTHAM
HOLMFIRTH
BLACK HILL
LONGDENDALE
BLEAKLOW
DENBY DALE
PENISTONE

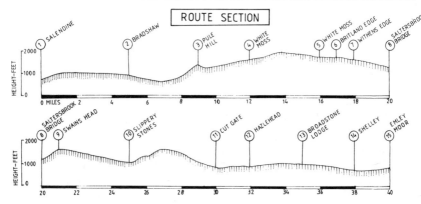

ROUTE SECTION

① SALENDINE ② BRADSHAW ③ PULE HILL ④ WHITE MOSS ⑤ WHITE MOSS ⑥ BRITLAND EDGE ⑦ WITHENS EDGE ⑧ SALTERSBROOK BRIDGE

HEIGHT—FEET
2000
1000
0

0 MILES 2 4 6 8 10 12 14 16 18 20

⑧ SALTERSBROOK BRIDGE ⑨ SWAINS HEAD ⑩ SLIPPERY STONES ⑪ CUT GATE ⑫ HAZLEHEAD ⑬ BROADSTONE LODGE ⑭ SHELLEY ⑮ EMLEY MOOR

HEIGHT—FEET
2000
1000
0

20 22 24 26 28 30 32 34 36 38 40

46

Don Morrison Memorial Edale Skyline Fell Race

Start and Finish — Edale
Distance — 22 miles (35 km) Ascent — 4700 feet (1435 m)
Category — Grade 'A'
Map — O.S. Peak District Tourist (one inch)
Organiser — Chris Worsell, Dark Peak Fell Runners
Current date — March

Introduction: Although the Edale Skyline has been a well known walk for some time it is now best known as the fell race, which originated in 1973 and is sponsored by Pam Morrison of Don Morrison Mountain Equipment, Sheffield. The race is organised each March under Amateur Athletic Association laws. A grade 'A' category designation has been given to the course by the Fell Runners Association which defines it as a Classic Fell Race — more than 250 feet gained or lost per mile, at least two thirds on fells, and very rugged. Only experienced runners are accepted who must have previously completed a long 'A' race. There is a 2 hours 30 minutes deadline to Mam Tor.

This circuit also makes an excellent walk. It is recommended that an anticlockwise approach is taken to ensure the most remote and wild part of the walk is covered early in the day.

Course Record: 2-35-16 by John Wild in 1982.

Further Information: Send a large SAE to E. A. Trowbridge 5 Kenwood Road, Sheffield 7.

Route Outline and Log:

No	Grid Ref	Checkpoint	Height feet	Distance mls	km	6mph pace	Date ....
1	122 860	Edale	900	0	0	0	....
2	109 867	Grindslow Knoll	1800	1	1.6	0.10	....
3	144 881	Jaggers Clough	1500	5	8	0.50	....
4	186 851	Win Hill	1516	8½	14	1.25	....
5	153 853	Lose Hill	1563	11½	19	1.55	....
6	127 835	Mam Tor	1695	13½	22	2.15	....
7	112 834	Lords Seat	1800	14½	23	2.25	....
8	083 851	Brown Knoll	1866	17½	27	2.54	....
9	079 861	Edale Cross	1750	18	29	3.00	....
10	109 867	Grindslow Knoll	1800	21	34	3.30	....
11	122 860	Edale	900	22	35	3.40	....

Total time ....

EDALE SKYLINE FELL RACE

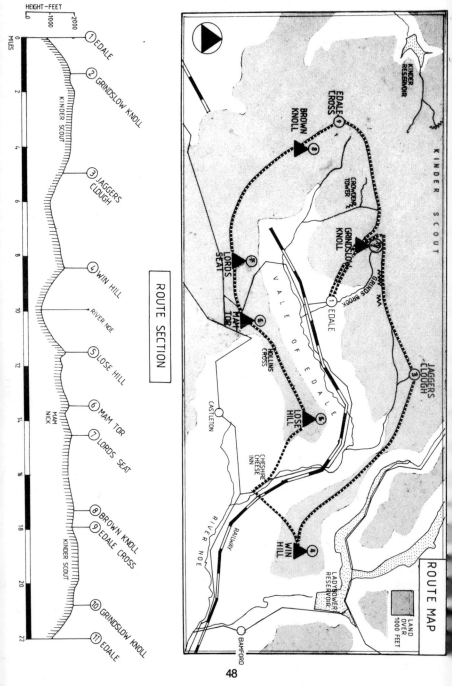

Marsden — Edale Trog Fell Race

Start — The New Inn Marsden (Grid Ref 050 115)
Finish — Railway Bridge, Edale (Grid Ref 123 853)
Distance — 22 miles (35 km)
Ascent — 3200 feet (985 m)
Category — 'A'
Map — O.S. Peak District Tourist (one inch)
Organiser — Bryan G. Stokes
Current date — December, 1st Sunday

Description: A winter fell race based on the Marsden-Edale classic (see page 8). There are stringent safety requirements and all entries are strictly vetted. Competitors may choose their own route, without trespassing, but must pass through intermediate checkpoints at the Woodhead Dam Wall (grid reference 082 994) and the Snake Inn (grid reference 113 906).

Course record: 2 hours 48 minutes by R. Pearson.

Further Information: Send a stamped addressed envelope to Bryan G. Stokes, 9 Charles Street, Sheffield 1.

Bog Dodgers Event

Time Limit — 12 hours
Current date — October
Organiser — Alan Earnshaw

Description: An event starting and finishing at Marsden Youth Hostel and based on the 22 mile, open, anytime challenge route (see page 17) and first staged in 1979.

Further Information: Send a large stamped addressed envelope to: Alan Earnshaw, Tourist Information Office, Brougham School, Brougham, Penrith, Cumbria, CA10 2AE.

Wild Ways Walk

Distance — **Approximately 20 miles (32 km)**
Area — Derbyshire
Organisers — **National Children's Home and West Derbyshire Ramblers' Association.**
Current Date — May, 2nd Sunday.

Description: First organised in 1971, this is a sponsored walk organised to benefit the National Children's Home. A different route is used each year with the opportunity to compete for two awards.

Further Information: Send a stamped addressed envelope for details of future Walks to Norman Witter, Regional Advocacy Director, National Children's Home, Princess Alice Drive, Chester Road North, Sutton Coldfield, W. Midlands, B73 6RD.

YHA Peak Marathons

The Peak Region of the Youth Hostels Associations has organised a variety of marathons since the 1960s based on Crowden Youth Hostel. In 1982 the event was staged in June and offered three routes:

50 miles: Crowden YH — Oyster Clough — Edale YH — Castleton YH — Hathersage YH — Moscar — Slippery Stones — Langsett YH — Salters Brook Bridge — Crowden YH.

35 miles: Crowden YH — Oyster Clough — Edale YH — Alport Bridge — Slippery Stones — Langsett YH — Salter's Brook Bridge — Crowden YH.

25 miles: Crowden YH — Oyster Clough — Edale YH — Alport Bridge — Slippery Stones — Langsett YH.

Membership of the YHA (see page 80) is necessary as the entrance fee includes overnight accommodation fees. Badges are supplied to successful participants. Running is not allowed.

Further Information: Send a large stamped addressed envelope for details of future events to: YHA Crompton Chambers, 55 Dale Road, Matlock, Derbyshire DE4 3LT.

Rotherham Advertiser Round Walk

Start and Finish — All Saints Square Rotherham
Distance — 25 miles (45 km)
Maps — O.S. sheet 111 (1:50,000)
Organiser — G. M. Rogers
Current date — May, 2nd Sunday

Description: A 25 mile circuit using local footpaths with many of the participants obtaining sponsorship to support local charities. Numerous individual and team trophies are awarded; badges are available to successful walkers. A 10 mile event takes place simultaneously. A folk concert is arranged on the previous evening.

Route Outline: Rotherham — Kimberworth Park — Wentworth — Upper Haugh — Parkgate — Valley Park — Wickersley — Spa House — Boston Castle — Rotherham.

Further Information: Send a stamped addressed envelope for details and an entry form after december to: G. M. Rogers, 367 Herringthorpe Valley Road, Rotherham 565 3AX.

Peakland Heritage Event

Time Limit — 12 hours
Current date — June
Organiser — Battyeford Scout Group

Description: This was first held in 1982 and is based on the 36 mile anytime challenge (see page 27). A number of indivdual and team trophies are awarded.

Further Information: Send a large stamped addressed envelope for an entry form to Mrs M. Hickling, School House, Stocksbank Road, Mirfield, West Yorkshire WF14 9QT.

Peakland Hundred

Start and Finish — Hayfield (Grid Ref. 036 869)
Distance — 100 miles (161 km)
Ascent — 9000 feet (2769 m)
Time Limit — 48 hours
Maps — O.S. Peak District Tourist (one inch)
Organiser — Long Distance Walkers Association

Description: Dick Chell and Haydn Morris spearheaded the organisation of this event in 1974 on behalf of the Long Distance Walkers Association. It was the second in a long line of hundreds organised by the LDWA which started with the Downsman in 1973 and currently ends with the Snowdonia Hundred in 1983.

Route Outline: Hayfield — Snake Road — Longendale — Wessenden Head — Flouch Inn — Ladybower — Fox House Inn — Rowsley — Monyash — Dovedale — Cat and Fiddle Inn — Goyt Valley — Hayfield.

Bolsover District Walk

This walk was first held in August 1982, modelled on the famous Nijmegen Marches in Holland. Organised by Terry Whetton and the Mansfield Branch of the Multiple Sclerosis Society there are two linear routes available covering 30 miles and 14 miles linking Bolsover Castle, Clowne, Creswell Crags, Hardwick Hall and South Normanton.

Further Information: Send a stamped addressed envelope to Mrs. P. Whetteon, 1 The Grange, Broadmeadows, South Normanton, Derbyshire, DE55 3ND.

Boscobel Walk

The 2078 (Boscobel) Squadron Air Training Corps organised the inaugural event in May 1982. Based on Codsall (north west of Wolverhampton), 40, 25 and 10 kilometre routes are offered following in the footsteps of King Charles II.

Further Information: Stamped addressed evelope with enquiries to Gerry Cooper, 69 Derwent Road, Palmers Cross, Wolverhampton, West Midlands.

Official Long Distance Footpaths and Recreational Paths

MILLERS DALE

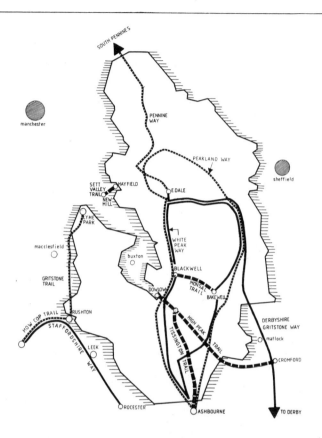

Pennine Way	270 miles	(423 km)
Peakland Way	96 miles	(154 km)
Derbyshire Gritstone Way	56 miles	(90 km)
Derbyshire Boundary Walk	280 miles	(451 km)
White Peak Way	80 miles	(129 km)
Paths in Adjacent Areas	Various	
Peakland Trails	Various	
Peakland Trackways	Various	

Pennine Way

Start — Edale, Derbyshire
Finish — Kirk Yetholm, Borders Region
Distance — 270 miles (423 km)
Ascent — 27000 feet (7925 m)
Maps — O.S. sheets 74, 80, 86, 91, 92, 98, 103, 109, 110, (1:50,000)
Links — Peak District: Peakland Way, Derbyshire Gritstone Way.
South Pennines: Calderdale Way. Yorkshire Dales: Centurion
Walk, Dales Way, Yoredale Way, Coast to Coast, Pennine
Link. North Pennines and Cheviots: Hadrian's Wall Walk,
Reivers Way.

Introduction: The Pennine Way probably needs little introduction. Officially opened on April 24th, 1965, as Britain's first long distance footpath, the concept first appeared in an article by Tom Stephenson in the *Daily Herald* on June 23, 1935. It then took 30 years of campaigning, and the provisions of the 1949 National Parks and Access to Countryside Act before the route became a reality.

Probably one of the first attempts on the walk was made by Major Clarke and a detachment of troops stationed in Edale in 1944. The Major found the featureless wilderness of Bleaklow and Kinder an ideal training ground, although not all of his troops shared his enthusiasm. One young soldier is reported to have remarked, 'If my mum knew I was in the charge of a blinkin' lunatic, she's go and see her MP about it.' During his stay the legendary Peakland walker Fred Heardman suggested to Clarke that he might undertake something really tough, a 250 mile walk from the Cheviots to Edale. Clarke and twenty eight of his troops took up the challenge. Six of them managed to reach Hebden Bridge after six days with only 38 miles to go. A seven day crossing was virtually in the bag when they were recalled for action over Arnhem, many never to return. A more recent crossing is that of the current record holder Brian Harney of Dark Peak Fell Runners and Rotherham Harriers which features in the *Guinness Book of Records.* Starting at 9 am on August 9th, 1979 Brian completed 113 miles in the first day, 81 miles on the second, 74 on the third and two miles on the forth, to finish in 3 days 42 minutes. A notable record has also been achieved by Geoff Bell, also of Dark Peak Fell Runners. Geoff completed a solo self-sufficient run, apart from water supplies, carrying 20lbs 11oz, 9lb 9oz of which was food. This took only 4 days 20 hours 44 minutes and was awarded the 'Achievement of the Year' trophy by the Bob Graham Club, membership of which requires completing 72 miles and 27000 feet of ascent over 42 Lakeland Peaks inside 24 hours!

PENNINE WAY

Over 10,000 crossings a year are now attempted; many succeed and many more fail! Whatever the outcome the route provides an unforgettable experience; a journey along the backbone of England, a tapestry of people, places, scenery, memories, challenges and rewards. The popularity of the Pennine Way should not disguise its difficulties. Within two miles of the pleasant meadows at Edale is the bleak featureless landscape of Kinder and Bleaklow which demands proven ability with map and compass, proper clothing and equipment and plenty of stamina.

Current Record: 3 days 42 minutes by Brian Harney.

Further Information: Badges and certificates are not issued.

Pennine Way Council: Exists to secure the protection of the Way and provide information to the public. In association with the Countryside Commission the Council publishes an accommodation list. A newsletter is published twice a year. For membership details send a stamped addressed envelope to Mr. R. Smith, 236 Lidgett Lane, Leeds LS17 6QH. For details of the accommodation list see references below.

References:

The Pennine Way, T. Stephenson (HMSO, 1981).
Pennine Way Companion, A Wainwright (Westmorland Gazette, 1976).
The Pennine Way, K. Oldham (Dalesman, 1983).
A Guide to the Pennine Way, C. J. Wright (Constable, 1977).
Walking the Pennine Way, A. Binns (Warne Gerrard, 1966).
A Walker on the Pennine Way, C. Walker (Pendyke, 1977).
The Pennine Way Pub Guide, Jowett, Mellor, Wilson. Send a stamped addressed envelope for details to P. Wilson, 76 Colne Lane, Colne, Lancashire.
The Pennine Way, T. Stephenson (Ramblers' Association). Send a stamped addressed envelope to Ramblers' Association, 1/5 Wandsworth Road, London, SW8 2LJ.
Pennine Way Accommodation List, (Pennine Way Council). Send a stamped addressed envelope for details to J. Needham, 23 Woodland Crescent, Hulton Park, Prestwich, Manchester, M25 8WQ.
High Peak, Byne and Sutton (Secker and Warburg, 1966).

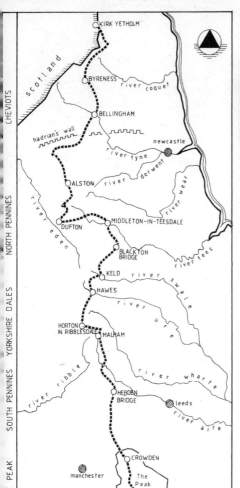

KINDER SCOUT

THE PENNINE WAY IN THE PEAK

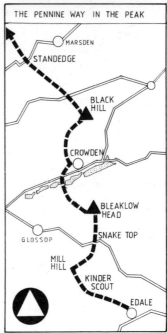

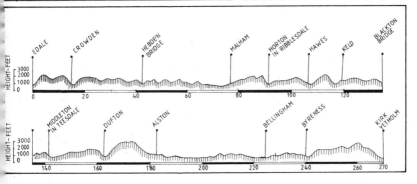

Route Outline and Log:

No	Grid Ref	Location	Height Feet	Distance mls	km	Date	Time
1	123 859	Edale	800	0	0	....	....
2	055 986	Crowden	725	15	24	....	....
3	972 265	Hebden Bridge	425	42	67	....	....
4	901 629	Malham	650	77	123	....	....
5	809 724	Horton-in-Ribblesdale	775	92	147	....	....
6	873 898	Hawes	800	107	171	....	....
7	893 012	Keld	1050	120	192	....	....
8	933 183	Blackton Bridge	950	135	216	....	....
9	947 254	Middleton-in-Teesdale	750	141	226	....	....
10	690 250	Dufton	600	162	238	....	....
11	717 462	Alston	900	183	292	....	....
12	839 833	Bellingham	378	225	360	....	....
13	771 024	Byrness	750	241	385	....	....
14	827 282	Kirk Yetholm	350	270	432	....	....

Total time ....

Peakland Way

Start and Finish — Ashbourne
Distance — 96 miles (154 km)
Maps — O.S. Peak District Tourist (one inch)
**   O.S. sheets 110, 119 (1:50,000)**
Links — Pennine Way, Derbyshire Gritstone Way, White Peak Way
Origin — John N Merrill, 1973

Introduction: A circular route which explores the full variety of Peakland scenery from the picturesque dales and villages of the White Peak to the gritstone edges and moorlands of the Dark Peak. The walk was devised by John Merrill, the well known long distance walker, lecturer and author.

Reference: *The Peakland Way,* John N. Merrill (Dalesman Books 1978).

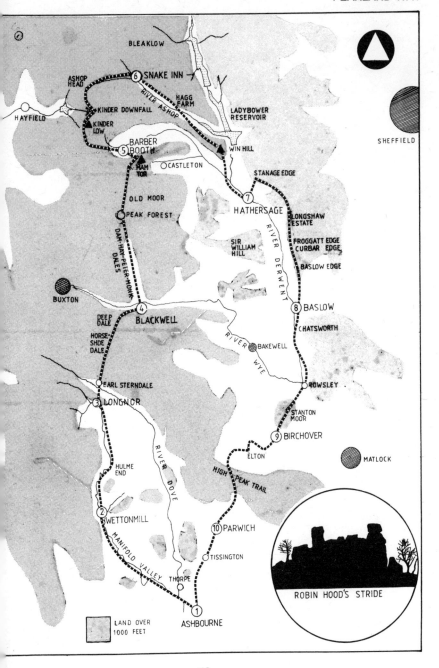

ROBIN HOOD'S STRIDE

Route Outline and Log

No	Grid Ref	Location	Height feet	Distance mls	km	Date	Time
1	180 465	Ashbourne	500	0	0	....	....
2	095 560	Wetton Mill	650	10	16	....	....
3	089 649	Longnor	950	17	27	....	....
4	127 720	Blackwell	1000	25	40	....	....
5	108 847	Barber Booth	850	36	58	....	....
6	113 906	Snake Inn	1050	45	72	....	....
7	230 815	Hathersage	550	57	92	....	....
8	252 723	Baslow	400	72	116	....	....
9	240 622	Birchover	800	81	130	....	....
10	187 554	Parwich	550	89	143	....	....
11	180 465	Ashbourne	500	96	154	....	....

Total time ....

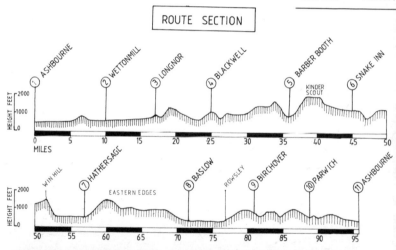

ROUTE SECTION

TOWARDS STANAGE (J. ALLEN)

60

Derbyshire Gritstone Way

Start — Derby
Finish — Edale
Distance — 56 miles (90 km)
Maps — O.S. sheets 119, 128 (1:50,000)
Links — Pennine Way, Peakland Way
Origin — Derbyshire Area Ramblers' Association, 1970

Description: This route which was devised in 1970 and eventually published as a contribution to Footpath Heritage Week in 1980. The walk takes a low level route through farmland following the River Derwent. At Chatsworth it then strikes up along the fine gritstone edges of the east before descending once again to the Derwent at Yorkshire Bridge. Here it ascends Win Hill and then takes in the impressive Lose Hill — Mam Tor Ridge on the way to Edale.

Easy to follow Wainwright type route maps are included in the guidebook. The walk may be attempted as a continuous excercise or in consecutive stages.

Completions: Badges are available for successful completions.

Reference: *The Derbyshire Gritstone Way,* Burton, Maughan, Quarrinton (Thornhill Press, 1980).

Route Outline and Log:

No	Grid Ref	Checkpoint	Height feet	Distance mls	km	Date	Time
1	352 365	Derby	150	0	0	....	....
2	350 451	Milford	250	8	13	....	....
3	331 543	Whatstandwell	240	17	28	....	....
4	309 590	Riber	750	21	34	....	....
5	307 655	B5057	1050	27	44	....	....
6	265 671	Beeley	400	31	50	....	....
7	260 747	Curbar Edge	1050	36	58	....	....
8	261 807	Burbage Bridge	1000	41	66	....	....
9	198 849	Yorkshire Bridge	550	48	77	....	....
10	124 856	Edale	770	56	90	....	....
						Total time	....

DERBYSHIRE GRITSTONE WAY

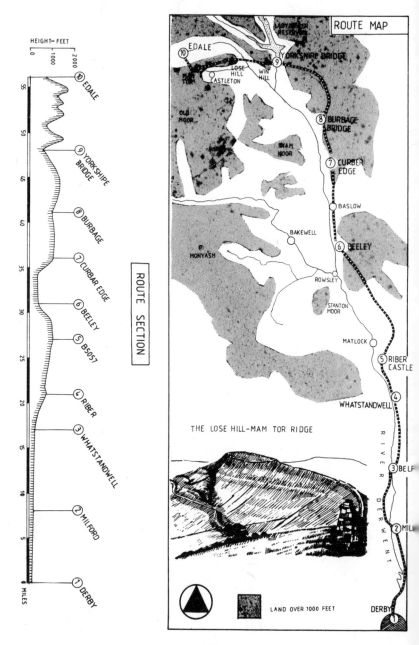

HEIGHT— FEET

ROUTE SECTION

ROUTE MAP

LADYBOWER RESERVOIR

⑩ EDALE
LOSE HILL
TOR
CASTLETON
WIN HILL
YORKSHIRE BRIDGE ⑨
OLD MOOR
EYAM MOOR
⑧ BURBAGE BRIDGE
⑦ CURBER EDGE
BASLOW
BAKEWELL
MONYASH
⑥ BEELEY
ROWSLEY
STANTON MOOR
MATLOCK
⑤ RIBER CASTLE
④
WHATSTANDWELL
THE LOSE HILL—MAM TOR RIDGE
③ BELP
②MIL
RIVER DERWENT
DERBY ①

LAND OVER 1000 FEET

⑩ EDALE
⑨ YORKSHIPE BRIDGE
⑧ BURBAGE
⑦ CURBAR EDGE
⑥ BEELEY
⑤ B5057
④ RIBER
③ WHATSTANDWELL
② MILFORD
① DERBY

MILES

Derbyshire Boundary Walk

Start and Finish — Sudbury Hall, Near Burton-upon-Trent
Distance — 280 miles (451 km)
Maps — O.S. sheets 110, 119, 120, 128, 129 (1:50,000)
Links — Pennine Way, Peakland Way, Derbyshire Gritstone Way
Origin — John Merrill, 1977

Description : This epic walk was undertaken by John Merrill in 1977. The route explores the full variety of Derbyshire scenery; the gritstone moors of the north; picturesque limestone dales: historic buildings and industrial landscapes.

Route Outline: Sudbury Hall — Rocester — Ilam — Hartington — Three Shires Head — Lyme Hall — Tintwistle — Withens Edge — Margery Hill — Longshaw — Chesterfield — Cresswell Craggs — Pleasley Vale — Hardwick Hall — Sandiacre — Swarkestone — Melbourne — Woodville — Burton-upon-Trent — Sudbury Hall.

Reference: *Peak District Marathons,* John N. Merrill (JNM Publications 1982).

White Peak Way

Start and Finish — Bakewell
Distance — 80 miles (129 km)
Maps — O.S. Peak District Tourist Map (one inch)
Links — Peakland Way, Derbyshire Gritstone Way
Origin — R. Haslam, 1982

Description: The latest addition to the Peak District's selection of long distance walks.

Route Outline: Bakewell — Elton — Ilam — Hartington — Ravenstor — Castleton — Hathersage — Bakewell.

Reference: *The White Peak,* Robert Haslam (Cicerone Press 1982).

Paths in Adjacent Areas

Sandstone Trail — Cheshire

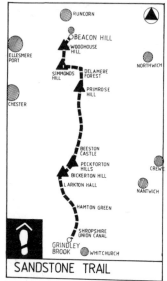

Start — Beacon Hill, Fordsham
Finish — Grindley Brook
Distance — 32 miles (51 km)
Maps — O.S. sheet 117 (1:50,000)
Origin — Cheshire County Council

Route Outline: Beacon Hill — Woodhouse — Alvanley Cliff — Simmonds Hill — Delamere Forest — Nettleford Wood — Fishergreen Farm — Beeston Castle — Peckforton Hills — Bickerton Hill — Larkton Hall — Hampton Green — Grindley Brook.

Reference: *Sandstone Trail Walker's Guide,* Cheshire County Council. Available from the Director of Countryside and Recreation, County Hall, Chester, CH1 1SF.

Gritstone Trail — Cheshire
(See page 66 for composite map)

Start — Lyme Park, Disley
Finish — Rushton, Cheshire
Distance — 18½ miles (30 km)
Maps — O.S. sheet 109, 118 (1:50,000)
Links: Mow Cop Trail, Staffordshire Way.
Origin — Cheshire County Council

Route Outline: Lyme Park — Sponds Hill — Brink Farm — Kerridge Hill — Tegg's Nose Country Park — Crocker Hill — Barleyford

Reference: *Gritstone Trail Walkers' Guide,* Cheshire County Council. (Address above).

Nottinghamshire Heritage Way (proposed)

Nottinghamshire Ramblers' Association are developing this route linking all the notable areas in the county, including Nottingham Castle, the University, Wollaton Hall, the Dukeries Newark and Southwell Minster together with places associated with D. H. Lawrence and Robin Hood. The distance will be approximately 150 miles and a guide will be published.

Enquiries to: Mr. C. G. Smith, 361 Nottingham Road East, Eastwood, Notts.

Robin Hood Way (proposed)

First conceived in 1980 by Chris Thompson of Nottingham Wayfarers' Rambling Club this route is now being developed to celebrate their Golden Jubilee of 1982. The Way starts at Nottingham Castle and finishes at Edwinstowe church and will be approximately 95 miles long connecting many of the places associated with Robin Hood. The official opening is anticipated in 1984.

Further information on the route can be obtained by sending a stamped addressed envelope to Roland Price, 23 The Hollows, Wilford, Nottingham NG11 7FJ.

Mow Cop Spur Trail — Cheshire and Staffordshire
(See page 66 for composite map)

Start — Rushton, Cheshire
Finish — Mow Cop, Congleton Edge
Distance — 6 miles (10 km)
Map — O.S. sheet 109 (1:50,000)
Links — Gritstone Trail, Staffordshire Way
Origin — Cheshire/Staffordshire County Councils

Route Outline: Rushton — Congleton Edge — Mow Cop.

Reference: *The Staffordshire Way – Mow Cop to Rochester,* Stafford County Council. Available from County Planning Officer, County Buildings, Martin Street.

Staffordshire Way

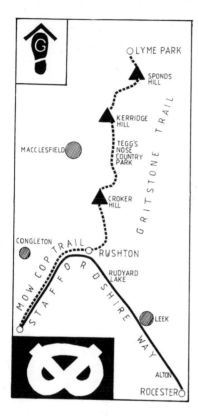

Start — **Mow Cop, Congleton Edge**
Finish — **Kinver Edge**
Distance — **90 miles (145 km)**
Maps — **O.S. sheets 118, 127, 128**
Links — **Gritstone Trail, West Midland Way, Worcester Way**
Origin — **Staffordshire County Council**

Route Outline: Mow Cop — The Cloud — Rudyard Lake — Cheddleton — Kingley — Rocester — Doveridge — Uttoxeter — Abbots Bromley — Colton — Shugborough — Cannock Chase — Kinver Edge.

References:
The Staffordshire Way, Staffordshire County Planning Department. Three booklets:
1. Mow Cop to Rocester
2. Rocester to Cannock Chase
3. Cannock Chase to Kinver Edge

Available from County Planning Officer, County Buildings, Martin Street, Stafford, ST16 2LE

Peakland Trails

THE following trails are all former derelict railway lines passing through varied countryside where visitors can enjoy long and short walks, cycling, pony trekking, nature study and picnics. Sections of these trails have been utilised in the Peakland Heritage Walk and Peakland Way. Leaflets are published as shown.

Tissington Trail — 13 miles

This is part of the former Ashbourne — Buxton line opened in August 1899 and closed in 1967. Following the purchase of the section by the Peak Park Joint Planning Board it was again opened in 1971 and 1972. It joins the High Peak Trail at Parsley Hay.

Reference: *Tissington and High Peak Trails* (Peak Park Joint Planning Board 1973).

High Peak Trail — 17½ Miles

This trail extends along the former Cromford and High Peak Railway, opened in 1830 and closed in 1967. The Peak Planning Board administer the 10½ miles within the Park from Daisy Bank via Parsley Hay to Dowlow near Buxton. Derbyshire Council manage the south-east section from Cromford.

Reference: *High Peak Trail* (Derbyshire County Planning Department, 1981). *Tissington and High Peak Trails* (Peak Park Joint Planning Board, 1973).

Monsal Trail — 8 Miles

Part of the former Midland line and one of the most scenic sections in the country it opened in 1863 and closed in 1968. As the line has numerous tunnels and viaducts it has been separated into four sections with link paths. The trail extends from Blackwell Mill Junction, three miles east of Buxton to Coombs Viaduct, one mile south of Bakewell, and includes the impressive Monsal Viaduct.

Reference: *The Monsal Trail* (Peak Park Joint Planning Board, 1982).

Sett Valley Trail — 2½ Miles

The Hayfield Railway was built for the Midland and Great Central Joint Railway Company and was opened in 1868. After it closed in 1970 it was purchased by Derbyshire County Council in 1973 and opened as a Trail between New Mills and Hayfield.

Reference: *Sett Valley Trail* (Derbyshire County Council Planning Department, 1981).

Peakland Trackways

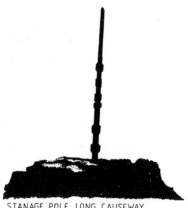

STANAGE POLE, LONG CAUSEWAY

Although walking is now regarded as a recreation and sport it should not be forgotten that for prehistoric man it was the only means of getting about. There is certainly abundant evidence of man's early wanderings in the Peak. Stone circles such as Arbor Low (161 636) and burial sites like Minninglow (209 572) and Harboro Rocks (243 554) were all linked by ancient trackways. The best known prehistoric track in the Peak is the Portway. Starting near Nottingham it passed through the eastern side of the Peak close to hill forts at Castle Ring (221 628), Fin Cop (175 709) and then branching to Mam Tor (128 836) and to Burr Tor (180 783) through Hope past Alport Castles (142 915) and Torside (077 965).

Later the Romans built roads across the moors: Long Causeway, Batham Gate and The Street are all good examples. The Dark Ages and Middle Ages then brought about numerous trade routes fostered by the establishment of markets; and later packhorse ways were developed to carry salt, wool and other commodities. Familiar checkpoint names like Edale Cross (080 861), Cut Gate (189 957), Jaggers Clough (150 877) and Hollins Cross (136 845) were even more significant to ancient travellers! A. and E. Dodd have undertaken a fascinating survey of the area which could make an excellent source of long distance walks.

References. *Peakland Roads and Trackways,* A. E. Dodd and E. M. Dodd (Moorland Publishing Company, 1974).

The Portway, an illustrated guide to the entire route, is to be published in 1983. Send a stamped addressed envelope with enquiries to M. W. Smith "Penmaen", 187 Chesterfield Road, Matlock, Derbyshire DE4 36A.

General Notes

BAKEWELL

NOE STOOL · KINDER

PARKHOUSE HILL UPPER DOVE

THE PEAK

Types of Long Distance Walking

Only walks of 20 miles or more have been regarded as long distance. Some walks marginally under this distance have been included if the route is of particular merit or a badge is available. For ease of reference the walks have been arranged into the following four categories which are generally characterised as shown:

Anytime Challenge Walks
- Can be attempted at any time.
- Specific route and distance to be completed.
- Route description, certificates and badges are often issued by a walk secretary.
- Route usually has to be completed as a continuous excercise, often within a time limit.
- Navigational ability essential.
- Essentially a challenge.

Challenge Events
- Date and start time are fixed.
- Entry by application form and fee.
- Maximum number of participants.
- Route is defined by a series of checkpoints where tallies must be punched.
- Rules to specify both equipment to carry and conduct.
- Certificate awarded for completion, badge often available.
- Individual and team trophies are often awarded.
- Time limit allowing all but the slowest to finish.
- Results sheet is usually published.
- Essentially a challenge although a competitive element usually exists.

Official Long Distance Footpaths
- Officially designated by the Countryside Commission.
- Specific Route.
- No time limits.
- Route is generally completed in several days of consecutive walking.
- Navigational ability is necessary.
- Route is waymarked with signposts and acorn symbols except over open county.
- Official guide is published.

Recreational Paths
- Route instigated by voluntary body, local authority or individual.
- Route is along existing rights of way.
- Completed either as a continuous excercise or in random sections.
- Guide is usually published.
- Navigational ability is necessary.
- Not usually waymarked unless instigated by a local authority.

Format of Walk Descriptions

An illustrated summary of all the established long distance walks has been included. In the case of annual challenge events which are organised on anytime, open challenge walks such as the Peakland Heritage walk, they have been included under both sections with relevant details shown under each section.

Each walk consists of the following sections where appropriate:

● Badge illustration, key information, introduction, completions.
● Further information — sources of further details of routes and entry forms; always enclose a stamped addressed envelope.
● References — these included all the published guides available and can often be obtained through booksellers. Prices and postage have not been given as these become rapidly outdated. Where an address is given, make an initial enquiry of the price, enclosing a stamped addressed envelope.
● Route map, route section, route outline and log. These relate to the key points on the route, maps are not to scale. In the case of challenge walks the route log gives a 2½ mph route schedule. This can be adopted to your intended start time to compile a personal route schedule. Arrival times can then be inserted to monitor progress and provide a permanent record. A typical route log might read as shown below:

Route Outline and Log:

No	Grid Ref	Location	Height feet	Distance mls	km	2½ mph Pace	Date 8.6.83
1	047 115	Marsden	600	0	0	0	.. 7.30 ..
2	075 072	Wessenden Head	1450	4	6	1.35	...9.10 ..
3	073 993	Crowden	700	11	18	4.25	..12.05 ..
4	088 929	Snake Road	1650	18	29	7.10	...2.43...
5	123 860	Edale	850	25	40	10.00	...6.20...
						Total time	..10.50...

Safety on Open Challenge Walks

1. A sound knowledge and experience of map reading, equipment and safety are necessary under conditions which can induce fatigue and impair judgement.
2. Devise a route schedule taking into account hours of daylight available and check progress against it.
3. In order to eliminate the risk of navigational errors, if possible survey the route beforehand in sections, making notes and taking relevant compass bearings.

4. If you have a support party ensure everyone knows precisely when and where you are to rendezvous. Failure of support parties to locate walkers can lead to rescue teams being needlessly called out. Arrange a central telephone point so that messages can be passed if you decide to retire, or inform the police so that time is not wasted looking for you.
5. Leave word of your route and make sure there are at least three people in your party.
6. Obtain a local weather forecast before setting out and be prepared for the worst; sudden weather changes are common.
7. Note the location of telephone boxes and possible escape routes.
8. The distress signal is six blows of a whistle or six flashes of a torch, both at one minute intervals.

Sponsored Walks

1. Sponsored walks in the countryside involving distances over 20 miles have become a popular means of fund raising. As such walks often involve individuals not accustomed to walking long distances it is essential all aspects of organisation and safety are fully considered. To this end the Ramblers' Association has published a booklet entitled: *Sponsored Walks in the Countryside.* For details send a stamped addressed envelope to the Ramblers' Association, 1/5 Wandsworth Road, London, SW8 2LJ.
2. The Madhatters is a club with the motto 'Achieve and Serve' which involves itself in undertaking strenuous activities in order to help worthy causes. Send a stamped addressed envelope to Peter Travis, 23 Kingsway East, Westlands, Newcastle, Staffordshire ST5 3PY.

Equipment for Challenge Walks

1. **Checklist**
   - Map and map case
   - Compass
   - Whistle
   - Walk schedule and pencil
   - Waterproof jacket and trousers
   - Woollen hat
   - Food to eat en route
   - Drink
   - Spare jumper and socks
   - Five pence pieces for telephone
   - Torch, spare batteries and bulb
   - Emergency rations
   - Polythene survival bag
   - First aid kit
   - Boots with patterned sole

2. Rules for challenge events specify precisely what is to be worn and carried. These should be strictly adhered to otherwise disqualification will result. In addition to the above items a mug and the exact contents of the first-aid kit may be specified.

3. The walks in this book are suitable only for experienced walkers with a sound knowledge of equipment and clothing needs. It is emphasised that equipment does not have to be costly; fashionable expensive gear does not make a good walker! Shorts, tracksuit bottoms, thermal long johns and waterproof overtrousers provide a combination that can be adapted to cope with all but the severest winter conditions.

4. Heavy boots with rigid soles and stiff uppers will probably be expensive, take a lot of breaking in and rapidly sap energy. Experienced walkers with strong ankles may find lightweight boots or strong trainers with a deep ripple or studded sole suitable for the Peak District. J. A. Jones (Mining), P.O. Box 8, Glossop, Derbyshire, SK13 9UP specialises in lightweight footwear; write for details.

Guidelines on Eating and Drinking

1. There are no miracle foods or drinks which make long hard walks seem like afternoon strolls! Practice, inherent ability and long-term bodily adjustment are more important factors in performance.

2. A general rule for eating during demanding walks is little and often so that the body does not become overloaded with the burden of digestion as well as muscular activity.

3. Generally the body is the best guide to immediate food and drink requirements. As muscle activity and sweat loss deplete the body of vital substances, preferences for types of food change. Foods which are readily attractive, palatable and digestable under normal conditions can differ from those required after fatigue has set in. Discovering which foods do or do not suit you is largely a matter of trial and error.

4. It is common knowledge that sweating is not just a matter of water loss. Salt tablets (sodium chloride) are often taken during hot weather to avoid cramp. However, potassium and magnesium are just as important as sodium. Specialist drinks are available which help replace body salts lost in activity. Staminade is a brand popular among some long distance walkers as it is available as a powder which can be mixed with water at convenient stopping points. It also contains glucose to aid energy output. Write for local stockists to Nicholas Laboratories Limited, Slough, SL1 4UA.

5. Sweet foods are usually consumed to assist energy output. Glucose is the fastest acting source of energy. The rule of little and often applies particularly to glucose and other forms of sugar, otherwise the body will over-react producing a low blood sugar level which will ultimately leave you feeling more fatigued.

GENERAL NOTES

6.   A common myth among active people is the need for plenty of protein. Several experiments have shown protein loss during activity to be no greater than when at rest. Eating protein will do nothing to aid performance; indeed, some nutritionists consider high protein intake, especially meat, to be damaging to health.
7.   Listed below are some of the more popular foods consumed during demanding walks:
●   Rice pudding and tinned fruit
●   Jam sandwiches
●   Salad sandwiches
●   Cake
●   Chocolate
●   Fresh fruit
●   Sweet tea
●   Staminade
●   Complan food drink
●   Glucose tablets

Reference: *Food for fitness* (World Publications, USA, 1975). Available from Running Wild, 2 Tower Street, Hyde, Cheshire.

The Peak District National Park

*Take nothing but photographs,
Leave nothing but footprints.*

Introduction: The Peak District was the first National Park to be designated in Britain in 1951 following the principles laid down in the National Parks and Access to the Countryside Act of 1949. Within its 542 square miles is some of the wildest and most beautiful country in England bounded on nearly all sides by the industrial towns of the north and the midlands. Even though it is a National Park the land is still in private ownership and other than open country, see page 75, there is no general right of access. The Park authority is empowered to protect and enhance the natural beauty of the area, and to promote its enjoyment by the public. Their work was recognised in 1966 when the Peak was awarded the Council of Europe's first Nature Conservation Diploma. This distinction, given initially for a five year term, has been renewed ever since; a reminder of the quality and importance of one of the most valued and yet still most vulnerable landscapes in Europe.

Information Centres:
- Bakewell, Old Market Hall — Bakewell 3227
- Castleton, Castle Street — Hope Valley 20679
- Edale, Fieldhead — Hope Valley 70207

Written Enquiries: Address these to The National Park Officer, Aldern House, Baslow Road, Bakewell, Derbyshire, DE4 1AE.

National Park Study Centre, Losehill Hall: This was established in 1972 to promote understanding, learning and interest in the Peak. Numerous professional, educational and holiday courses are arranged. For further details write to; Peak National Park Study Centre, Losehill Hall, Castleton, Derbyshire, S30 2WB.

Accommodation:
- Camping barns — four camping barns have been established in the Peak. They are Losehill Barn (near Losehill Hall), Alport Castles Barn, Abney Barn (near Ivy House Farm) and One Ash Grange Narn (near Lathkill Dale).
- *Camping and Caravanning in and around the Peak District* (Peak Park).
- *Accommodation and Catering Guide* (Peak Park).
- Hagg Farm Youth Hostel (open to non-YHA members) and camp site.

Publications: An extensive range of books and leaflets is available from the National Park Office including general information, accommodation (see above), official reports, *Peak Park News,* the quarterly journal of the Peak, and *First and Last,* a superbly illustrated guide to the Peak. For a full list of publications write to National Park Office, Baslow Road, Bakewell Derbyshire, DE4 1AE.

The official guide *Peak District National Park,* published by HMSO, is currently (March 1983) out of print.

Access to Open Country

History: The rambling movement emerged at the turn of the century with the Sheffield Clarion and Rucksack Clubs being founded. At that time the Derbyshire moors were closely guarded by the landowners who wished to preserve their shooting interests, and Water Board bailiffs concerned with the purity of drinking water supplies. The access movement gathered momentum and annual rallies where held in the Winnats Pass from 1926. Conflicts with gamekeepers were inevitable and culminated with the historic 1932 Kinder Mass Trespass. Another 17 years of campaigning took place before the 1949 National Parks and Access to the Countryside Act was passed. The Peak District National Park was set up in 1951 and access agreements were negotiated with landowners which still require substantial annual compensation payments regardless of any damage caused. Today 76 square miles of moorland are covered which represents over 60% of all Access land in the country. While the battle for access is being won in the Peak, at a price, the Ramblers' Association is still pressing for more effective legislation to give the general right of access to open country which is enjoyed in much of Europe.

Areas of Open Country: Kinder, Bleaklow, Langsett, North Longendale, Chew; White Path Moss (Stanage); Froggatt, Curbar, Baslow and Bubnell (Eastern Edges).

Closures: In order to accommodate the shooting interests of the landowners, access areas may be closed for up to twelve days during the grouse shooting season (August 12th to December 10th). A monthly list of closures is published and signs are erected at access points on the day(s) when a moor is closed.

References:

Access Map – 1" Kinder, Bleaklow, Longendale (Peak Park).
Access Map – 2½" Eastern Edges and Stanage Edge (Peak Park).
The Story of Access in the Peak District, P. Rickwood (Peak Park, 1982).
The 1932 Kinder Trespass, B. Rothman (Willow Publishing, 1982).
Freedom to Roam, H. Hill (Moorland Publishing, 1980).
High Peak, Byne and Sutton (Secker and Warburg, 1966).
Open Country: Public asset or private domain, Brief for the Countryside No. 9. (The Ramblers' Association, 1982, available from 1/5 Wandsworth Road, London SW8 2LJ.

Public Transport

Peak District Public Transport Timetable — Published by Derbyshire County Council, County Planning Department, Public Transport Unit, County Offices, Matlock, Derbyshire DE4 3AG. Also available from Peak Park Information Centres. A comprehensive bus, coach and rail service timetable of all operators in the Derbyshire Peak District and adjoining parts of Chesire, Staffs and South Yorkshire.

Scheduled Railway Services — enquire at your local station about the following services:

Sheffield — Hope Valley — Edale — New Mills.
Buxton — Whaley Bridge — Newton — Stockport — Manchester.
New Mills — Marple — Romiley — Manchester.
Hadfield/Glossop — Broadbottom — Manchester.
Matlock — Cromford — Ambergate — Belper — Derby.
Macclesfield — Stockport — Manchester.
Manchester — Greenfield — Marsden — Huddersfield — Leeds.
Sheffield — Penistone — Huddersfield.

Peak Wayfarer — A one day ticket covering most bus and rail services within the Peak District, and also services to and from anywhere in the Manchester area. On sale at bus, rail and information centres in the Peak and Manchester areas. Or write or phone: Greater Manchester Transport, 2 Devonshire Street North, Ardwick, Manchester M12 6JS, Tel: 061-226 8181.

Day Rover — A date-it-yourself one day ticket covering most bus and train services within West Yorkshire and providing access to north-eastern tip of the Peak from Marsden, Meltham and Holmfirth. Write for details to West Yorkshire PTE, Metro House, West Parade, Wakefield, WF1 1NS.

Public Service Timetable Pack — published by the Peak Park Joint Planning Board and available through information centres, or by post from their National Park office at Bakewell.

Countryside Commission

1. The Countryside Commission was brought into being under the 1968 Countryside Act when it assumed the functions of the National Parks Commission set up in 1949. Its powers were enhanced by the 1974 Local Goverment Act and in 1982 it achieved independent status. Matters relating to long distance footpaths, National Parks, Areas of Outstanding Natural Beauty, Heritage Coasts, recreational routes and public access all fall within its responsibilities.

2. The following publicity leaflets are currently available together with a publications list. Write to John Dower House, Crescent Place, Cheltenham, Glos. GL5 3RA. (telephone Cheltenham 21381).

● *Long Distance Footpaths and Bridleways* – an illustrated leaflet on all the approved paths.

● *Recreational Paths* – a county by county summary of some of the long distance routes which have been sponsored by County Councils, voluntary organisations and individuals.

● *The Pennine Way* – an illustrated leaflet of the route.

● *The Countryside Commission* – a brief explanation of its functions.

● *Countryside issues and action* – a prospectus setting down policies and priorities.

● *National Parks of England and Wales* – an illustrated leaflet describing all ten National Parks.

● *Public Transport in the National Parks* – a very general summary of public transport facilities..

Local Authorities

Although the Peak Park Joint Planning Board is responsible for administering the National Park, local authorities are responsible for countryside recreation in the adjacent areas. All of them have countryside divisions specialising in matters such as recreational paths, rights of way, countryside parks, guided walks, countryside ranger services, promoting associated public transport schemes, information centres and publications. Contact the following addresses:

Cheshire County Council, Countryside and Recreation Division, County Hall, Chester, CH1 1SF. Chester 603390.

Derbyshire County Council, County Planning Department, County Offices, Matlock, Derbyshire DE4 3 AG. Matlock 3411.

South Yorkshire County Council, Department of Recreation, Culture and Health, John Vernon House, 70 Vernon Road, Worsbrough Bridge, Barnsley, South Yorkshire S70 5LH. Barnsley 82216

Staffordshire County Council, County Buildings, Martin Street, Stafford, ST16 2LE. Stafford 3121

West Yorkshire Metropolitan County Council, Recreation and Arts Division, County Hall, Wakefield. Wakefield 367111.

Nottinghamshire County Council, Planning and Transportation Department, Trent Bridge House, Fox Road, West Bridgeford, Nottingham N62 6BJ. Nottingham 842 842.

Organisations

Long Distance Walkers' Association

The LDWA was founded in 1972 by Alan Blatchford and Chris Steer. Although it encompasses all categories of long distance walking, it caters primarily for those interested in challenge walks. There is now a dedicated following of over three thousand members with local groups in most parts of the country including the High Peak, West Yorkshire and Staffordshire. Ten one hundred mile challenge walks have been organised in all parts of the country including the Peak. One of the main attractions of membership is the newsletter appropriately called *Strider* edited by Chris Steer. A comprehensive calendar of challenge events is included together with general articles and news of local group activities.

For membership details send a stamped addressed envelope to the LDWA Membership Secretary, 4 Mayfield Road, Tunbridge Wells, Kent, TN4 8ES.

Ramblers' Association

The RA has played an important role in the creation of both official long distance paths and recreational paths. It also works to preserve the footpath network and secure access to open country; conserve our natural heritage against encroachment; oppose harmful legislation and helps promote recreational walking.

Membership includes receipt of their magazine *Rucksack,* a comprehensive bed and breakfast guide and details of local walk programmes. Send a large stamped addressed envelope to The Ramblers' Association, 1/5 Wandsworth Road, London SW8 2LJ.

Fell Runners' Association

The FRA exists to encourage and foster better standards of fell running and allied mountain racing throughout the United Kingdom. Some ten races are organised in the Peak. Membership includes the receipt of *The Fell Runner* magazine and a fell running calendar of events. For details send a stamped addressed envelope to Norman Berry, 165 Penistone Road, Kirkburton, Huddersfield HD8 0PH.

British Orienteering Federation

Write for details to BOF, National Office, 41 Dale Road, Matlock, Derbyshire, DE4 3LT.

Compass Sport magazine, incoporates the official magazine of the BOF together with reports on fell running and wayfaring. Send for details to Ned Paul, 37 Sandycoombe Road, Twickenham Middlesex TW1 2LR.

Youth Hostels Association

The YHA was founded to help all, especially young people of limited means, to a greater knowledge and care of the countryside. This is done by providing hostels and simple accommodation throughout the country. A number of long distance challenges are organised by the YHA. Write for membership details to YHA, National Office, St. Albans, Hertfordshire, AL1 2DY.

Council for the Protection of Rural England

(Sheffield and Peak District Branch)

Founded in 1924 the CPRE has played an immeasurable role in conserving the peace and beauty of the Peak District. The establishment of a National Park in the Peak is due to the work of the CPRE as well as the purchase of many notable areas which were presented or covenanted to the National Trust. Send for membership details to CPRE (Sheffield and Peak District Branch), 22 Endcliffe Crescent, Sheffield, S10 3EF.

Open Spaces Society

Founded in 1865, the Society aims to promote knowledge of the law so that paths and commons may be preserved for the public benefit. Send a stamped addressed envelope to 25A Bell Street, Henley-on-Thames, Oxon, RG9 2BA.

Peak and Northern Footpath Society

Formed in 1894 the Society continues to protect the footpath network of the Peak and adjacent areas. Send a stamped addressed envelope to Mr. D. Taylor, 15 Parkfield Drive, Tyldesley, Manchester, M29 8NR.

National Trust

Founded in 1895 the Trust owns or protects over 50 square miles of countryside in the Peak District, the most notable acquisition being Kinder Scout itself in 1982. Send a stamped addressed envelope to The National Trust, 42 Queen Anne's Gate, London, SW1H 9AS.

Mountain Eye

Photographer, lecturer, adventurer, and former Rucksack Club President, John Allen offers a comprehensive slide lecture and advisory service. Contact: John Allen, 10 Rainow Road, Macclesfield, SK10 2PF. Telephone Macclesfield (0625) 612291.